Yes! I Am Catholic

Yes! I Am Catholic

How Faith Plays a Role in My Life

Beth Dotson Brown

Saint Mary's Press®

Genuine recycled paper with 10% post-consumer waste. 3451

The publishing team included Laurie Delgatto, development editor; Lorraine Kilmartin, reviewer; prepress and manufacturing coordinated by the production departments of Saint Mary's Press.

Printed in the United States of America

ISBN 978-0-88489-964-8

Library of Congress Cataloging-in-Publication Data

Dotson Brown, Beth.
   Yes! I am Catholic : how faith plays a role in my life / Beth Dotson Brown.
   p. cm.
ISBN 978-0-88489-964-8 (pbk.)
   1. Catholics—United States—Biography. 2. Catholic
Church—Apologetic works. I. Title.
BX4670.D68 2007
282.092'273—dc22
[B]

                                            2006100164

Dedication

I dedicate this book to my husband, Jim, my family, my friends, and all the health-care professionals who helped me become physically healthy again as I was writing this book.

Author Acknowledgments

There are so many people who have kept me in their prayers during the past year that I cannot name them all, but you know who you are and that it has been your prayers that carried me through.

I want to especially thank my parents, Paul and Vera Lee Dotson, who have always supported my desire to write. Dad, you got me started on my publishing journey by providing me with an idea for my first published magazine article when I was a teenager. And Mom, you are the best unpaid researcher and public relations person a writer could have! Also thanks to my brothers, David and Dan, and my niece, Morgan, who all bring happiness into my life.

My husband, Jim, is a constant source of encouragement, as well as a brainstorming partner, critic, and proofreader when I ask him to be. His friendship and love help cushion the rejections and celebrate the acceptances.

Thanks to the members of the Grassroots Writers Group and the House Writers, both of which have given me practical advice as well as space for dreaming.

Kudos to the nurses at the Markey Cancer Center Chemotherapy Lab. When I showed up with my laptop, ready to work, you took care of me with gentle expertise. Your interest in my writing made me feel that the words would reach their audience.

I appreciate the diligent work of my editor, Laurie Delgatto. Thank you for shepherding this project and teaching me about book publishing.

Many people offered suggestions about folks that I might interview. I would like to thank the following people who helped me set up interviews: Mark Andel, Helen Barr, Lin Billingsley, David Dotson, Vera Lee Dotson, Carla Durand-Demarais, Brooke Gabris, Sr. Eileen Golby, Pat Griffin, Liz Kelly, Julie McCarty, Judy Milford, Mary Claire Mingus, Claire Mugavin, Mike Penich, Sr. Robbie Pentecost, Fr. John Rausch, Maria Ruiz Scaperlanda, Casey Sterr, Susan Sucher, Carrie Swearingen, and Bill Tougaw.

And, finally, I must express my gratitude to everyone who agreed to be interviewed for this book. These are your stories, and ultimately it is your generosity in sharing them that will touch our readers. Peace to you all.

Contents

Introduction

Ask and you shall receive.

Anyone who has gone to church has heard that sentiment. Although it is a favorite of mine, at times I have found it to be deceptively simple. There have been occasions when I asked and did not receive, or so it seemed.

There have also been times when I received even before I knew what to ask for. Such was the case with this book. The offer to write it came to me just when I most needed to hear stories of faith.

Seek and you shall find.

Although I was facing a personal health crisis, I spent time in silent prayer, trying to open myself to answers from God and guidance about who to interview for this book.

God told me to knock and the door would be opened. So it was.

I made a list of people that I might interview and invited them to share their stories. I began to ask simple questions: Why do you choose to be Catholic? What do you like about your faith? Each person I spoke with opened the door and gave me answers.

One of the first stories that truly inspired me was that of Helen Barr, a fashion business owner in New York City. She had faced repeated tragedies in her life, including the aftereffects of the 9-11 terrorist attack on her business and the death of her sister from cancer. Yet she said it was her faith that sustained her. Even when she did not know what to do from minute to minute, she remained open to hearing God's guidance, and God took care of her.

I interviewed my uncle and godfather, Bill Tougaw. I knew that he had left the Church for a significant period of time in his life, but I did not know why or why he had returned. He shared that story, as well as the four words from the Our Father that have gotten him through the most difficult times in his life: thy will be done.

I talked with actress and Olympic gold medalist Tara Lipinski as she prepared for an acting audition. She told me about her devotion to Saint Thérèse the Little Flower and the miracles God had wrought in her life through the intercession of this saint. I marveled at her story about the workings of one of my favorite saints in her life. And I remembered the power of prayer.

Each of the people I interviewed opened the door to their faith life so that all of us might take away a bit from their stories to strengthen our own journeys. They certainly did that for me. My soul became richer as it filled with the stories of these people, people who could be your next-door neighbor, favorite athlete, beloved author, or special teacher. God sent me an answer to a prayer I did not know I had, and I am all the richer for it.

As you read this book, I hope these stories will have some of the answers you are seeking. Turn the page and the door will be open.

1

my faith
sustains me

It is often a moment of crisis that causes people to understand the importance of their faith. They nearly accomplish a lifetime goal, only to fall short of it; a loved one dies; terrorists attack. People realize that they were sustained by faith during the crisis.

derek parra

Derek Parra says that building a relationship with God is like building any other relationship; it takes time and commitment. For him, part of the building process has been spending time with the Scriptures and talking to God. "Once you feel comfortable with that connection," he says, "it's like having Mom and Dad to help you and kiss the boo-boo. God can do the same thing in God's own way."

Derek Parra,
Olympic Medalist, Speed Skating

Derek Parra was raised Catholic in a Mexican-American home in California. He faced his share of troubles at a young age, when his parents divorced. He left home when he was seventeen years old to pursue a skating career.

"I always believed in heaven and God and everything like that, but it wasn't until I was away from home that I developed a personal relationship with God," Derek recalls.

He began developing that relationship while he was living in a trailer without electricity near a training facility in Wisconsin. He did not have any money, but his coach found him work and helped him continue to train. Living in the middle of the woods, Derek struggled with loneliness. During this time a pastor handed him a Bible.

> "I started reading it, and that's when I developed a personal relationship with God."

"I started reading it, and that's when I developed a personal relationship with God. This relationship reinforced my faith. From that point on in my life and in my career as a skater, God played an important role. When I had hard times, I didn't look at them as hard times but as times when God was teaching me something. I was learning something from the experience that would help me in another part of my life."

When Derek found himself without money, food, or work, "somebody came out of nowhere to help me." It happened too many times, he says, for it to be coincidence. Rather, he believes it was God working in his life.

Derek took his faith and his experience with him to Nagano, Japan, in 1998, when he earned a spot on the U.S. Olympic speed skating team. Just as he was perched on the brink of achieving one of his goals, his name was pulled from the starting list because of a clerical error. "I was devastated and didn't know what to think," Derek says.

He returned to the United States for four more years of training. At the 2002 Olympic Games in Salt Lake City, his name stayed on the roster. Then it rose to the top. Derek won the gold medal in the 1500-meter race and set a world record in the process. He won the silver medal in the 3000-meter race.

Looking back on the Nagano experience, Derek can now say: "I think I wasn't prepared back then to win. I wasn't prepared as a person to handle everything, and that experience allowed me to grow. I came back after four more years of training and growing up as a person. I ended up being able to handle everything that happened at that time. With God's grace, I was successful and won the gold medal and went out and preached to others about my faith and talked about it freely. Maybe that's why. Maybe I was chosen to win because of what I would do and how I would share my faith."

Faith continues to be the foundation of Derek's life. He believes that the faith Catholics share makes them all one family. He calls on his Church family as he continues to train. "Maybe that's something I enjoy the most because I'm living in Utah and my family is in Florida when I'm preparing for the games. When I am lonely, when I'm feeling alone, I can call anybody I know at the church. I can go to church and I can call the pastor and talk, and it's like being home."

"When I had hard times, I didn't look at them as hard times but as times when God was teaching me something. I was learning something from the experience that would help me in another part of my life."

helen barr

Helen Barr did not always rely on the Catholic faith that sustains her today. Although she was raised Catholic, she drifted away from the Church for a number of years. As a young person, she thought that people who were religious must be plain, unaccomplished folks. Today Helen is neither plain nor unaccomplished, but she considers herself a devout Catholic.

Helen Barr, Fashion Business Owner

As an adult, Helen listened to the Reverend Norman Vincent Peale. She heard something in his sermons that helped her develop a personal relationship with Christ. As she learned that the Holy Trinity was always available in her life, she also found an example of faith to admire. Helen began volunteering with the Missionaries of Charity in the South Bronx, where she met Mother Teresa. "My experience with the Missionaries of Charity, probably more than anything, changed my life because I witnessed faith in action and the extraordinary love of these women," Helen says.

> "My experience with the Missionaries of Charity, probably more than anything, changed my life."

When she returned to the Church, Helen developed a new appreciation for the Catholic Mass. "The Catholic Church has created a Mass that lets us begin by confessing our sins, to feel cleansed. It moves us on to glorify God and profess our faith again, together. And we are prepared to receive the sacrifice that Jesus made for us in the Eucharist," Helen explains.

We feel "physically and spiritually changed by having received the Body of Christ. When our experience as a community has been completed, we leave with an inner sense of peace and strength. Every part of the Mass is significant in uniting us with God."

Helen deepened her faith by taking part in silent retreats in Assisi and by reading the writings of Saint John of the Cross and Saint Augustine. She greatly needed this faith when life threw her a series of unexpected challenges.

While Helen was running a fashion business with a partner in New York City, her sister died of breast cancer, leaving a thirteen-year-old daughter. Helen adopted her niece, instantly becoming a single parent with a great new responsibility. "Without my faith, I don't know how I could have withstood so many challenges," Helen remembers.

The challenges did not end there. When Helen's business partnership dissolved, she lost all the company assets, including her retirement fund. "I had no money, and I had a teenager to raise," Helen remembers. "That's when my faith deepened tremendously. I would pray every hour for strength as I started my own business. Hour by hour I rebuilt my life; it would have been completely impossible without my faith. I would have quit. I simply would have sat in tears. My faith changed everything."

Half of the companies in her building went bankrupt after the terrorist attacks of 9-11. "My faith was a deciding factor in staying in business," Helen says. "Every day through my prayers to God, I knew that I would find a way to solve problems sometimes so insurmountable that I honestly didn't know what I would do four hours ahead. I stayed calm and prayed and knew the answers would come. And they did."

Helen finds inspiration and examples of perseverance in historical personalities, such as Winston Churchill, but she says those examples are not enough; they must be combined with faith. "The strength to keep going, the belief, the smile on my face when I wasn't very happy—that was from knowing I wasn't alone. It was knowing God would see me through. It was praying every hour.

"Some of those things were so tragic that without the strength of knowing there's something more, it would have been impossible," Helen says. "The reward is astonishing because each time you are tested, you realize that God is so remarkable and you experience a different aspect of God's mercy and it's astonishing. Everywhere you look, God's there, if you look. God's the net. You can leap and know that the net is there."

Helen Barr lives her faith outwardly in the workplace. "In my office, we pray in the morning. We're not all Catholics, but we pray. That was a hard decision to make." Another outward sign of her faith is her financial support of the Missionaries of Charity. "God has given me so much, and I should honor that," she says. "There should be a light that shines from what I'm doing."

fr. robert pittman

"The Catholic faith is a very sustaining faith. My faith is telling
me that God is in control, God loves me, God is caring for me,
and I have nothing to worry about."

Fr. Robert Pittman, Priest, Blessed Sacrament Congregation

When Fr. Robert Pittman was six years old, in church with his mother, he realized that he wanted to be a priest. "There were many, many seemingly impossible obstacles, but inside of me, I felt as though this is what God wanted me to do, and I was going to be able to do it.

"We were growing up extremely poor, almost homeless and foodless and everything else, living on our grandfather's farm for survival. Mom had had a bad experience, and she was trying to raise us the best she could. One of the things she was very strong about was raising us in the faith."

> "There were many, many seemingly impossible obstacles, but inside of me, I felt as though this is what God wanted me to do."

It was not easy at that time to be African American and Catholic. "When I was growing up, certainly the segregation and the treatment of black people in church were very disedifying to me," Father Pittman says. "Members of my faith were practicing the opposite of what we're taught." Father Pittman could see that although people professed their Catholic faith, they did not always put it into practice. "But still, I felt that I had to stay with it. By abandoning my faith, I wasn't going to gain anything." Father Pittman says that for him, the core of faith is loving one's neighbor as oneself.

When he was old enough to attend the seminary, Father Pittman had to leave Maryland and go to Mississippi. "Mississippi was a long ways off. I had heard all kinds of stories about the things they did to black people in Mississippi and that it was a horrible place to go."

Nonetheless, he went, only to be called home to help his family before he finished school. He worked so hard at home during those years that he compromised his health, and the seminary would not allow him to return. The diocese would not take him either. So Father Pittman looked for another avenue and found the Congregation of the Blessed Sacrament. They accepted him. "These struggles seemed impossible, but God took care of them in God's own way. That's why I take the principle that if God doesn't give you what you want, God always gives you something better."

> "If God doesn't give you what you want, God always gives you something better."

Since his ordination, Father Pittman has served in Africa, England, and the United States. Many of his dreams have come true. "I wanted to go to Lourdes; I wanted to go Fátima; I wanted to do this and do that. So many of those things sooner or later were realized. Look, I'm here, I'm in Fátima, in Lourdes, in the missions. I'm studying Portuguese in Lisbon. I dream about it, and the next thing I know, it's happening. If you open your eyes and pay attention, you are blessed over and over."

Father Pittman continues to be blessed and to work as he approaches the age of eighty years. He ministers at the Body of Christ Farm in Maryland and travels to Mozambique to help the Church there. "Some people say I'm too old to go back to Mozambique, which somewhat makes sense because I am rather old, but at the same time, I believe I have a mission there. There's some work there that God wants me to do, and God will see me through."

Forgiveness is an important concept in Fr. Robert Pittman's life. "One of the sermons I preach often is on forgiveness, how important it is that we forgive from the heart. It's only when we forgive that we can enjoy peace and the assurance of God's forgiveness."

timothy goebel

Timothy Goebel grew up in the Catholic Church, with a devout Catholic mother and a father who was not Catholic but attended church with the family. Timothy says of his faith: "It's something that's always been a part of my life, and it's something that I feel plays an important role in my life. I try my best every day to live my faith, to be a good person and a good example of morals and values for other people."

Timothy Goebel,
Olympic Medalist, Figure Skating

Timothy's faith has been especially important to him in his career as a figure skater. "Being in the career I'm in right now with skating or being in any sport where there are so many external demands on an athlete's time is a challenge. When I'm in the limelight, I'm always expected to be 'on' and be sort of perfect all the time, to fulfill the role people expect me to fulfill. It's really easy to get caught up in that and be completely consumed by my career."

"I've had some rough times these past few years. My faith has helped me stay on track and appreciate that everything is not always wonderful in life. It's what you make of the hard times and what you learn from them that helps you get through them."

While Timothy was training full-time for the Olympics, eight hours a day, his faith was important to him. "It's easy for me to get so wrapped up in and focused on one thing that I sort of let the rest of life slide," he says. He believes it is important to "keep a good perspective on things and not get too up when things are going well or despair too much when they aren't." Timothy's faith is the force that helps him maintain that perspective.

At times Timothy has despaired. He won the bronze medal in the 2002 Olympics but struggled in the 2003–2004 season. He was dealing with equipment issues and injuries and was working with a coaching staff that did not encourage or support him. While he was going through that difficult time, he was living and training across the country from where his parents lived.

"It was a really, really hard time for me. I think part of what helped me get past my problems, refocus, and find the motivation to keep training and trying to improve was my faith. At that point, I didn't have a lot left. The only thing I had to fall back on was my faith."

"I've had some rough times these past few years. My faith has helped me stay on track and appreciate that everything is not always wonderful in life. It's what you make of the hard times and what you learn from them that helps you get through them." Timothy emerged from those times a disciplined person. He was on his way once again to pursuing his dream of Olympic gold. When he encounters difficulties, he remembers that his faith tells him that Jesus Christ provided a human example of sacrifice and love, an example of how we all should live.

Besides winning the bronze medal in the 2002 Olympics, Timothy Goebel placed second in the U.S. Nationals in 2005, placed second in the World Championships and won the Cup of China Grand Prix in 2003, and placed first in the U.S. Nationals in 2001.

2

prayer helps me communicate with God

They pray when walking, attending Mass, listening to music, reading the Scriptures, or sitting quietly and appreciating the beauty of nature. Through prayers, Catholics receive answers, comfort, and fortification of faith.

catherine hicks

Catherine Hicks is effusive about her love for the Catholic faith, even the parts that are difficult. "It's deep, it's dark, it's shiny, it's happy, it's magical, it's tough, it's real, and it's old. It was founded by Christ himself. I love that it goes back to the Last Supper. I love that it's a mystical religion, very prayer and meditation oriented."

Catherine Hicks, Television Actress

Hicks was raised in the Catholic Church. She has found that her faith has comforted her. As a child, she loved the idea that Christ was her friend. "As I got older and was alone as a young professional woman, I knew I could go [to my faith] if I was scared or lonely," Catherine says.

Catherine still likes being in Church today. "I love the spirituality, the peace and quiet of the Church. I love that churches often have statues and candles. It's very comforting," she says.

When Catherine travels, she finds it reassuring that wherever she goes in the world, the Church is there and she can find a Mass to attend. "I love that it's international," Catherine says. "I love that it's not just white Americans. It's everywhere; it's global."

"Catholics pray hard. Catherine describes the Church as mystical, meaning that "you seek the faith of God through prayer."

In addition to being globally accessible, the Catholic Church is a prayerful Church. "Catholics pray hard," Catherine says. She describes the Church as mystical, meaning that "you seek the faith of God through prayer, and the more you pray, the more you see God and the more [God responds]. It's like a relationship."

Catherine attends Mass as often as she can, enjoying the opportunity to listen to the Scriptures. She finds that focusing on the Scriptures during Mass is easier than reading them at home. At Mass she encounters one of the great mysteries of the Church that leaves her in awe: "We have the Eucharist. God became visible in human form and lives on in bread [and wine]. It's forever mysterious."

Besides praying at Mass, Catherine likes to pray the rosary and recite memorized prayers. "It's hard to make up your own prayers," she says. "I love that there are so many wonderful prayers to be learned. It makes it easy to pray. I often pick out a memorized prayer."

The saints also offer Catherine opportunities for prayer. "I love the saints, the real people who have died and are in heaven, whom we can talk to," Catherine says. "There are a lot of heavenly friends."

Some of Catherine's heavenly friends are her patron saint, Saint Catherine of Laboure, Saint Thérèse the Little Flower, and Saint Joseph. "I love Saint Anthony [the patron saint of lost things]. He bails me out at least five times a day because I'm left-handed and I lose everything," she says. "Even my Protestant husband is devoted to Saint Anthony."

What is the result of all the prayers? Catherine sees "the soul as a muscle. One needs to work out for one's physique, and one needs to work out for the soul by praying. By praying, we exercise the soul. The soul gets in better and better shape all the way toward seeing the face of God."

Catherine sees "the soul as a muscle. One needs to work out for one's physique, and one needs to work out for the soul by praying."

Catherine believes that people are not praying enough. She teaches her daughter about prayer. She thinks it is important to raise the question "Why are we here?" even with young people.

As one ponders the possibilities, it is necessary to back up one's beliefs and prayers with actions. Catherine thinks the Catholic Church does a good job with this through organizations such as Catholic Relief Services and the Saint Vincent de Paul Society. "Catholic charities are everywhere," Catherine says. "The Church really lives Christ's mandate to feed the hungry and clothe the poor."

"There's extreme devastation on the planet," says Catherine, as she muses about Africa and other war-torn places. "There's plenty to focus on. Catholicism is a socially active religion that works with the poor." The Church also stands up for people who are oppressed, she says.

Catherine believes in being active in one's local community too. "We have to visit a neighbor, that old person down the street. We've got to be kind," she says. "Be nice to the kid who is 'left out.' Why? Because God created that person."

Catherine Hicks has appeared in numerous movies and television shows. She played the role of Annie Jackson-Camden in the series *Seventh Heaven* from 1996 to 2007. In 2005 she became the spokesperson for Catholic Relief Services on the Darfur situation in Sudan.

bill tougaw

Church is not the only place where Bill communicates with God. "I do that through prayer, trust, and accepting whatever God's will might be. I can look outside and see the beauty of nature, and God's there. I leave the house in the morning and trust that [God will] get me home at night. The communicating might not be in silent or spoken prayer with words. It's in knowing that God's presence is there."

Bill Tougaw, Retired Trucking Manager

Bill Tougaw was raised Catholic and attended Catholic schools. He played basketball for a Catholic university during his college years. When he divorced at age twenty-nine, however, he drifted away from the Church. He had two children and feared that if he got an annulment of his marriage, his children would be labeled "illegitimate."

He moved forward with his life, carrying his Catholic roots with him and respecting the faith but not attending Mass. He married a woman who had also been divorced, and together they created a family with his two children, her daughter, and a son they had together.

For about twenty-eight years, Bill stayed away from the Church, exploring other options. "I would go to other churches and leave feeling empty," he remembers. He felt that other faiths were less rooted in the truth and more likely to blow with the wind. When he thinks about the Catholic faith today, he says: "It's not willy-nilly. It won't always be politically correct. It's stable and steadfast. It won't be different next week."

> When he thinks about the Catholic faith today, he says: "It's not willy-nilly. It won't always be politically correct. It's stable and steadfast. It won't be different next week."

Catholic doctrine, he points out, is set in stone. And when he hears what the Church has to say about issues such as abortion, he says, "You can depend on this: It will not change. I respect that, and I count on it."

When Bill learned more about the meaning the Church attaches to annulment, he felt more comfortable about going through with the process. "I wanted to get involved again [in the Church] because I felt as though I was missing something."

While he waited for the annulment to be granted, he began to attend Mass again. "During that time, I went to church weekly, wishing especially to be able to receive Communion. The urge for that got stronger and stronger." Bill says about the Mass: "When I don't go, I feel as though I've committed a sin against myself because not going deprives me of an important opportunity. The Mass refreshes and renews me for the following week."

Church is not the only place where Bill communicates with God. "I do that through prayer, trust, and accepting whatever God's will might be. I can look outside and see the beauty of nature, and God's there. I leave the house in the morning and trust that [God will] get me home at night. The communicating might not be in silent or spoken prayer with words. It's in knowing that God's presence is there."

> "God gave me the confidence I needed; I went from being a wreck who was about to lose it to having the confidence I needed to get through. I wish everyone could experience that."

When Bill's father was near death, communicating with God helped Bill get through the difficult time. His father had cancer, and his health was failing. One night the doctors told the family that his father probably would not make it through the night. Bill's parents had been married for forty-five years; although Bill's mother looked as though she was doing okay, Bill was worried about her and his sister.

Bill did not know what to do. So he turned to a prayer he had known all his life. "I prayed the Our Father over and over again," he says. "I had probably prayed it about nine times when I started concentrating on the line 'thy will be done.' As I said it, this warmth grew in my chest. I started to feel almost weightless. God gave me the confidence I needed; I went from being a wreck who was about to lose it to having the confidence I needed to get through. I wish everyone could experience that."

Bill found comfort in those words and in his faith when his wife died in a freak accident. "I kept going back to those four words: 'thy will be done.' They are as powerful as anything."

Bill knows that his actions show his faith, so he tries to live by the Golden Rule and be a good example. "I'm proud of my Catholic faith." Bill has married again, and says, "I'm proud that my wife, Brenda, is taking instruction and becoming Catholic."

It has been a meandering journey for Bill Tougaw, but it is obvious from his stories, enthusiasm, and example that he is comfortably at home in his Catholic faith again.

Bill Tougaw says he has great respect for priests, in spite of the negative publicity they have gotten in recent years. "The true priests continue to be proud of being priests, and they do their duty for God and their flock." His own parish priest sat with him by his dying wife's bedside from 2:30 a.m. until 6:00 a.m. "He was there when we needed him. That was a real gift to us."

paula davis

Paula Davis grew up as the seventh of twelve children in a Catholic family. Her parents taught her about the faith. "We said prayers together as a family, and [the pastor] would come over to pray over us all the time," she remembers. She treasures a photograph of herself and her siblings with their priest when she was still the baby in the family.

Paula Davis, Housekeeper, Xavier University

Paula Davis grew up as the seventh of twelve children in a Catholic family. Her parents taught her about the faith. "We said prayers together as a family, and [the pastor] would come over to pray over us all the time," she remembers. She treasures a photograph of herself and her siblings with their priest when she was still the baby in the family.

Paula's father was a sergeant in the army, and her mother stayed home and took care of the children. "I think they did a beautiful job bringing us up in the Catholic faith. My mother had to go through a lot." The children attended Catholic school until the tuition got to be too costly to keep all of them there. Paula's brothers sang in the church choir. She thinks back on those early days of being ingrained in the faith and says: "That's really all I knew. I was raised [Catholic], so I stuck with it."

Although she does not have anything against other churches, the Catholic Church is where Paula feels at home. "I love the teachings of the Church and lots of different things," Paula says. "There's just something about it I like. I also like that the Catholic faith hasn't changed." The steadiness of the Mass, the teachings, and the traditions reassures Paula.

> "There's just something about it I like. I also like that the Catholic faith hasn't changed."

One of the childhood traditions Paula continues to practice is praying. "I try to pray every day and go about things the right way. It's so rough out here." Paula is aware of her environment because she walks thirty minutes every night to get home from her job as a housekeeper at Xavier University in Cincinnati. She finds those walks to be a good time to pray.

35

She says three prayers in the evening. "I love the Our Father, and I love the Hail Mary. I like a lot of them. And the 'Lord, Lay Me Down to Sleep.' That's something I've prayed since I was a kid."

When Paula prays the Our Father, she is praying for her brothers and the men of the world. The Hail Mary is offered for her sisters and the women of the world. The 'Lord, Lay Me Down to Sleep' is for her seven granddaughters. "And I pray for the world to be a better place. Those prayers have so much meaning."

Paula learned to pray from her parents. She says that even if people are not brought up Catholic, they can still learn to pray such prayers. "Talk to someone who's really into the faith to learn how to pray," she suggests. She also thinks it's a good idea to read the Bible.

> "Even if people are not brought up Catholic, they can still learn to pray such prayers. Talk to someone who's really into the faith to learn how to pray."

Working with a boss who is a minister of another faith sometimes brings up questions of religion. She remembers that at one point, her boss noticed all the difficulties that were coming her way: the death of one sister from cancer, the loss of two nephews, the deaths of her parents, and the loss of a sister who had a baby. Her boss asked her how she dealt with all the losses, and she answered: "I pray. I have to pray for some sanity."

Paula has experienced things she cannot explain except through faith. She remembers one particularly bad period in her life when she was lying in bed and felt a big gust of wind around her that pinned her to her bed. It frightened her deeply. "I pulled myself up and went and laid on the couch; I laid by Jesus's picture, and the feeling went away." She cannot define what happened at that moment. Years later she still remembers the terror, followed by the comfort Jesus gave her.

"Some people say that when you pray, your prayers aren't answered, but I'm a living witness that they are. I've prayed a lot of prayers that have been answered." For example, Paula remembers a time when she desperately needed help to pay her gas and electric bills. She got the money she needed. Recently she was in a housing situation that made her unhappy. When she began to look for a new place, the rental expenses discouraged her. "One day I got out of bed after I had been praying and praying; I started walking and just lucked upon a place. God is good!" The new place was larger than anything she had expected to be able to afford, and it was close to her job.

If someone asks Paula about her Catholic faith, she is glad to tell them how she feels. "I just love it because it's a beautiful faith," she says.

Paula Davis especially likes to pray the rosary. In 2002 Pope John Paul II enhanced this Catholic devotion by adding a new mystery. To the traditional meditations on the joyful, sorrowful, and glorious mysteries, he added the mystery of light, which highlights some of Jesus's actions on earth.

matthew ott

Matt was raised Catholic, but he did not consider himself to be truly Catholic until his Confirmation. "It's when I said for myself: this is what I believe. I'm glad I was given the opportunity."

Matthew Ott, Student, College of Saint Benedict

When Matthew Ott was five years old, he saw a television program about the needs in Africa and heard the song "Amazing Grace" playing in the background. Looking back on that time from his perspective as a college student, he remembers thinking, "What I'm gonna do when I grow up is become a football player and make a lot of money and buy a helicopter and go over there and bring all of them over here." He laughs at the idea now, but adds, "It was kind of extreme, but it definitely had a big impact on what I'm doing today."

Now that Matt is a student at the College of Saint Benedict in Minnesota and living away from his family, he still practices his faith. "It's who I am. It's part of my life," he says. "God has revealed to me who he is, the shepherd, and who I am, a sheep in the fold. God created me and God loves me. [Jesus] died in my place and then rose from the dead. I rejoice and revel in God's love for me, knowing that God is alive, knowing that God's love is unconditional. This joy is my faith and practice."

> "It's who I am. It's part of my life. God has revealed to me who he is, the shepherd, and who I am, a sheep in the fold. God created me and God loves me."

With classes, homework, service work, socializing, and so much more, college students have much in their lives that can distract them from God. Matt tries to stay on track with daily prayer, which he calls a way of communicating with God. Prayer enriches his life, helps him make decisions, and leads him to put his faith into action in a variety of ways.

Matt began discovering different methods of prayer when he was in high school. He once took a backpacking trip alone that he describes as being like a Native

American vision quest. The purpose was "to kind of turn thoughts inward so you can really see who you are. Because if you don't know who you are, then you really can't know who your Creator is. Once you find out who you are, you might be able to see some of the fingerprints or markings of your Creator." Matt recommends this getting-away quest for anyone who wants to really think about things.

Matt says of his prayers, "I just kind of talk with God." He tells God what is going on in his life, apologizes for mistakes he has made, and asks for help. He also reads the Scriptures, where he finds reassuring words about God's love and wisdom.

"I like reading prayers that have been written too," Matt says. "I feel that some people who are seasoned in the journey of faith can help me along in my journey if I read what they have to say."

> "I just kind of talk with God." He tells God what is going on in his life, apologizes for mistakes he has made, and asks for help. He also reads the Scriptures, where he finds reassuring words about God's love and wisdom.

Matt also says, "I write in a journal, and that helps me go further with my thoughts."

Music is part of Matt's prayer life. He says that when he listens to Christian music, "it seems like every song is a prayer. That's a big part of my faith journey, as well."

Matt's faith journey includes wanting to do good for others. "I try to work to improve the lives of others," Matt says. The work might mean contributing money, time, or organizational efforts. He participates in the campus ministry at the College of Saint Benedict. He draws on memories of how he felt when he was five years old and learned about the needs in Africa. He got some of his fellow students to contribute five dollars each a month to sponsor a child in Uganda. "It would cost too much for one college student alone to sponsor a child," he says. "But a group of students can do it."

"I have an awareness of God's presence and love in all life experiences, so my decisions are influenced by God," he says. He calls on the spirit of counsel to lead him to the right decision.

Having a strong base of faith helps Matt through the difficulties all students face: examinations, pressures, and depression. "I have a hope that carries me through the toughest times," he says.

"My faith brings meaning to life. I love and cherish the gift of life God has given me. To know God and to begin to fathom God's power and love and might and mercy is fulfilling. God's love is more than enough."

Matthew Ott believes that prayer is primary to his work. The Benedictine Sisters, founders of the college he attends, affirm that with their motto, *Ora et Labora,* which means "pray and work." Matt believes that God is glorified by the work he does.

bishop thomas gumbleton

"It's my way of relating to God," Bishop Thomas Gumbleton says about his Catholic faith. "I'm very grateful for my faith life, which comes to me through the Church."

Bishop Thomas Gumbleton

"It's my way of relating to God," Bishop Thomas Gumbleton says about his Catholic faith. "I'm very grateful for my faith life, which comes to me through the Church."

As a priest since 1956, Bishop Gumbleton has carried his faith into many arenas and is especially well known for his work for social justice. He founded the peace group Pax Christi and served as president of Bread for the World. He has traveled extensively around the world and won a long list of awards.

His faith originated in a devout Catholic family. "Catholic devotional practices were very much a part of our life," he says. "We learned to say prayers at an early age. We said prayers at home, then of course at school, and in religious education. It was a given in my family that we were Catholic and we would always be Catholic."

Today he says about his Catholic faith, "It's so much a part of the whole fabric of my life that it's just there, in a sense, when I need it."

Prayer is the link that makes faith and connection to God available to Bishop Gumbleton. "The most important thing is how I have learned to be in communion with God through prayer," he says. "I've learned how to pray through the Scriptures and be with the word of God and let the word of God be with me. And of course there's the public prayer of the Church, which I also find inspiring when we celebrate the public liturgies."

> "The most important thing is how I have learned to be in communion with God through prayer. I've learned how to pray through the Scriptures and be with the word of God and let the word of God be with me."

For Bishop Gumbleton, the best time for quiet reflection and prayer is first thing in the morning. He has found great reward in quiet prayer. "It's a beautiful way to pray. It's a formative way to pray. Not only am I speaking to God but I'm listening to God, and that's what changes me. That's what prayer should do. Prayer isn't to change God; prayer is to change us. That happens when we begin to listen to God," Bishop Gumbleton says.

"God is unchangeable, literally and totally. We're the ones that have a need to keep on growing into the full people God intends us to be. The way we do that is by a listening form of prayer."

As a priest, Bishop Gumbleton works daily to be a servant of the people, which to him means trying to serve as effectively as possible. "As a minister, I'm to be formational and lead people into a fuller awareness of God and their relationship to God. And also a fuller awareness of what God has called us to do."

> "God is unchangeable, literally and totally. We're the ones that have a need to keep on growing into the full people God intends us to be."

He disagrees with the philosophy that God will call us to something extremely difficult that will be a sacrifice. "Yes, there might be sacrifice involved." For example, there are times when people give up certain things they would like to do because they have to study, earn a degree, and graduate in order to move into the field to which God is calling them. But by entering into oneself and reflecting on one's gifts and inclinations, Bishop Gumbleton says, "God will lead you to a place of peace and fulfillment."

For example, becoming a priest is not without sacrifice and hard work. Nonetheless, Bishop Gumbleton says, "When I was ordained, I experienced the deep love of God, that God would call me to do such a thing."

Ultimately, a lifetime of service and prayer has led Bishop Gumbleton to say, "I still believe that the Catholic Church is a continuation of the community of disciples that Jesus first gathered together when he was on earth and began his own public ministry.

"Being a Catholic for me is the best way I can connect with God. I connect through Jesus, the Son of God but also our brother. Being part of his community of disciples—that's what I find to be a great blessing—and the privilege of sharing his mission together. God sent Jesus, and Jesus sends us."

Bishop Gumbleton often endorses significant causes and has participated in acts of civil disobedience, fasts, and prayer vigils. In addition, he has appeared on television and radio, and in documentary programs such as *Bishop Against Bombs,* which was released in March 2003.

catholic values guide my decisions

3

I n conscious and subconscious ways, faith guides the decisions of Catholics every day. Whether decisions are about voting in Congress to go to war or about what time to get home to be with the family, they are part of daily life. When Catholics make decisions, they show what Catholics value.

jim wayne

Although Jim Wayne was raised a Catholic, he realized at some point in his life that he did not have to continue to practice the faith. "It's definitely a conscious decision."

Jim Wayne,
Social Worker and Kentucky State Legislator

"What I've recognized is that faith is a gift I've been given. I can choose to accept the gift or ignore the gift. What I've been doing is trying to pay attention to the gift and accept it as openly as possible. Part of my reason for doing this is that faith is such an integral part of who I am as I interact with the world around me. It shapes everything."

What Jim's faith shapes are the choices he makes daily. He tries to center his day in prayer to give him the perspective he needs. Instead of spending his morning watching television or reading the newspaper before he rushes out into the world, he says, "There's sacred time that I have every day." For him, it must be a minimum of fifteen minutes. He does not use formulaic prayer during that time; he prefers to sit in silence. He sometimes jump-starts his sacred time by reading a short passage from the Scriptures or other spiritual writings. Then he puts the reading aside and breathes deeply.

Instead of spending his morning watching television or reading the newspaper before he rushes out into the world, he says, "There's sacred time that I have every day."

Another thing that shapes Jim's day is his priorities. He puts his wife and marriage at the top of the list, with his other family members next. His obligations to them supersede all other obligations. "It's a matter of priorities that my faith helps me to frame; my first priority is my marriage vows," he says.

Jim uses his faith in his work as a clinical social worker and Kentucky state leg-islator. For example, some days he drives from his home in Louisville to the state capitol, Frankfort. On one day, he recalls, "I wanted to stay connected to God in a conscious way." So he did not turn on the radio in his truck. When he arrived in Frankfort and gave his presentation, he realized that "those moments in the truck had helped me gain perspective." His faith often provides guidance about issues he champions, such as affordable housing. "I'm involved in [various issues] because I'm motivated by my faith."

Part of what helps Jim do this is his membership in a community of believers. "I hope all Catholics will realize that their faith is not just their own personal journey; it's done in the context of a community of believers who have a long history of sort-ing through how God works with human beings.

"To me, the sacraments, especially the Eucharist, are very important. The Eucharist is kind of the ultimate expression and celebration of God's presence in our midst," Jim says.

"At Mass, we take our lives and we offer them to God as a community. "

Jim enjoys reading the Scriptures and listening to homilies that connect the Scriptures to modern-day life. Jim says: "At Mass, we take our lives and we offer them to God as a com-munity and then God transforms us to be Christ in this world right now. And we are united with Christ in one body through Communion. It's a powerful dra-ma of God's dance with human beings."

Jim sees that paying attention to the evil in the world is important. The Church teaches the faithful about issues such as war and capital punishment. "Especially in America, we don't want to listen to what the Pope says about some of these issues. But if we do, we realize that God is much bigger than America. If we're going to tune in to God and God's plan for the human race, it means looking at war as something evil. It means looking at capital punishment as something evil and then standing up and saying something about that and acting on that."

"Communion. It's a powerful drama of God's dance with human beings."

To be able to respond to the evil in the world, Jim says, it is imperative that people take time for prayer and reflection. He tries to pray and reflect on the choices he makes daily. His faith, he says, "gives me a certain sense over time of inner peace that I know for sure can't be found anywhere else."

"I see all of life as a gift from God. God is constantly trying to pull me into a relationship." Without that relationship, Jim says, life would be a void. "It's kind of the center of everything."

Just as people have routines for physical health, Jim Wayne says, his prayer routine is for his spiritual health. "I'm not always successful at that; sometimes the distractions take over. But yet I've tried."

matt smith

Everyone has to make important decisions in their lives. For Matt Smith, there was a time when he was making such decisions in front of millions of people. He spent two seasons with MTV's reality show *The Real World*. He understood that certain decisions would win the applause of the other cast members and give the show better ratings. But he also knew that he had been raised as a Catholic, and he wanted to give witness to his faith.

Matt Smith, Cast Member of MTV's *The Real World*

"When I was in the middle of filming the TV show, I had a lot of temptations, sexual temptations and temptations to use drugs and alcohol and temptations to try to be someone I'm not or to behave in a way that I was not taught," Matt says. "All of those things add up. Those were critical decisions that I had to make, and I had to make them knowing there would be millions of people watching me."

A bonus of being Catholic, Matt says, is that when it came time to make choices, he could ask himself what Jesus would do and use the answer to guide him. And so he did. He once turned down the chance to attend a party with the cast because it was at the Playboy mansion, a place he believed encouraged sinful behavior.

> "The times when I try to follow Christ's teachings are the times I have the most joy, the most peace, and a real sense of comfort."

"The times when I try to follow Christ's teachings are the times I have the most joy, the most peace, and a real sense of comfort," Matt says. "If I look to the world around me for advice, it's not going to happen. But if I look toward the Gospel, that's where the real truth is. It gives me guidance."

Matt also finds guidance in the oral and written teachings of the Church, which present Catholics with a way of living. He finds nondenominational or interdenominational practices lacking because they are based solely on an individual and his or her Bible. Matt recognizes that the Bible will help him in ways he cannot imagine, but he also acknowledges that Catholics do not believe that the Scriptures alone are their guide. "Christ founded a Church, not a series of people with their bibles," Matt says.

Matt chooses to look to the Church for guidance in his everyday life rather than to society. "I've lost faith in the collective consciousness of society," he says. "I look around and see that we're so oversexed and self-centered and self-serving. I can't count on society to tell me what is right and what is wrong."

> "Just because I want to do something doesn't mean God wants me to do it. It's always when I look for God's will in something that I am most satisfied."

Matt also does not rely on popular music to guide him. He thinks it can lead people to being self-centered, so he prefers to listen to praise and worship music.

One way Matt tries to discover the difference between right and wrong is through contemplative prayer. For many years, he thought that living out his faith depended on how many times he could pray each day and how often he attended Mass, said the rosary, or used other devotional practices. He has discovered that another way to approach living his faith is to do everything peacefully in the presence of God.

One aspect of this is trying to be at peace with what God calls him to do. "Just because I want to do something doesn't mean that God wants me to do it. It's always when I look for God's will in something that I am most satisfied," Matt says. "In small decisions and big decisions, I try to step closer toward God because when I do that, I know God's also taking a step toward me."

Whether Matt is deciding what to buy or when to wake up or whom to spend time with, he is open to God's guidance. "Almost always people are trying to guide us for their gain and not for our gain or well-being. I know with Christ and the Church Christ gave us, it's a matter of guiding us to the place that will bring us the most peace."

"I've lived in the middle of everything," Matt says. "I've met almost every band that I ever listened to in high school. I've met almost all the actors that I've admired. I've hung out with all the models. I've ridden in the fastest cars and been at all the parties. I've done all that and in all that everyone was trying to guide me in one direction or another. I have seen so much heartache and so much brokenness, not just in Hollywood but in people's lives in other places." These experiences have caused Matt to learn that "I'm not supposed to do this on my own. When I follow the Lord, it's a totally different way of living."

Through his Internet ministry, Matt tries to provide the same kind of universality and community for teens. His experience with MTV has taught him about the power of the media, so he's trying to use that for a good cause. He's especially interested in reaching out to those who are isolated from other Catholic teens.

Matt has found the Catholic Church to be a crucial companion on his journey. "Anything that survived two thousand years has to have something going well for it. I've heard people say that if you look at the history of the Catholic Church, it's obvious that only God could have kept it together. I just have to have faith in that."

Matt Smith takes comfort in knowing that he is not the only person who follows Catholic teachings in his life. He loves the universality of the Catholic Church. He grew up in north Georgia, where his family drove to another county to attend church and he was mocked for his faith. He now finds that when he travels across the country, he likes knowing that the same Scripture readings are being proclaimed in every Catholic Church each week, "one county over, one country over, and on the other side of the globe. It's just so cool."

steve chabot

In a rapidly changing world, Steve Chabot draws comfort from the fact that he can count on the Church to stay steady. "When the Church does change, the process is generally very deliberative."

Steve Chabot, United States Congressman

Steve is part of a government body that makes decisions for the country, the United States House of Representatives. The Catholic faith in which his parents raised him helped form the values that he uses in his work. "I have the privilege of addressing some major moral issues in Congress," Steve says. "The pro-life issue is a good example. I'm strongly pro-life."

Growing up in a Catholic family and attending Catholic school formed the morals Steve carries through life. "As an adult, I try to listen attentively at Mass to what the priest says — the Gospel, the sermons. I personally like it when [the homilist] emphasizes such things as protecting unborn life."

Even though Steve relies on his faith to guide him, he does not always agree with the teachings of the bishops and the Pope. When he disagrees, he sometimes asks questions to determine if he is interpreting the teachings as they were intended.

His convictions are especially important, he says. "When I have to vote on life-and-death issues, such as whether to support military action, I really do some soul searching to decide what is morally right. Those are times when my faith is probably being tested."

The issues Steve faces all relate to how a person treats others. He believes this is an important foundation of the faith. "Jesus is clearly the standard by which we all should measure what we do in this world. Jesus is

"When I have to vote on life-and-death issues, such as whether to support military action, I really do some soul searching to decide what is morally right. Those are times when my faith is probably being tested."

the perfect example of how we should try to live our lives and what principles we should follow. I will be held accountable for the way I live my life and the way I've treated my fellow human beings on this earth."

Steve hopes he is passing on those values to his own children. "There's a consistency to [the faith]; there's something you can depend on," he says. "Catholic values help us realize that there are important things in life other than just making money or being successful. It's important that we care about our fellow humans, that we have responsibilities in life other than being successful or gaining acclaim or getting material things. That's what the faith teaches."

Steve Chabot was one of the twenty-six members of Congress who attended the funeral of Pope John Paul II in Rome. It was the first time he had been to Rome and the first time he had seen a pope. "That was one of the most significant experiences I've had in a long time," he says. "It was very moving."

larry clark

Growing up in a strict Catholic environment at home and in school, Larry was on "a steady diet of Catholicism." Like many boys, he was an altar server at Mass. But for a short time after he graduated from college and before he married, he did not attend Mass every Sunday. He felt guilty. Eventually, he began to attend Mass again. "I suddenly was going to Mass because I wanted to go. From that point on, I would go because I wanted to go, and sometimes more often than once a week."

Larry Clark, Retired Businessman

Larry Clark understands the guilt some Catholics feel if they do not go to church, as well as the peace that returns when they feel drawn back.

Larry practices his faith in his home life and his work life. He thinks that respect for others, belief in God, and trying to live a good life are the most important goals in life. "There are always challenges in married life and in raising children. I have a very supportive wife who's also Catholic," he says. "When we have challenges, we always turn to [the Church], and there's always some consolation there."

"When we have challenges, we always turn to [the Church], and there's always some consolation there."

Some of that consolation has come when someone died or was going through a difficult time. "It seems like any time things get tough and we aren't as strong as we think we can be, I get very humble and go right back to my faith and ask for help. I think it sometimes can help me find a way to get through the situation and determine the solution."

Larry drew on his faith during his career in sales, a competitive field. In the business world, Larry encountered many people who were devious rather than ethical. "My religion taught me to choose what was right and not to worry. I wouldn't be able to be unethical in my business life. I'd have a hard time sleeping at night," he says. "I always wanted to win. I was fortunate enough to win doing it the right way."

At one point, Larry discovered that a competitor was outperforming his company by using unethical practices. He did not like what he saw, and asked his staff, "what do you guys think?" It was a fantastic meeting because everybody agreed they were not interested in doing it the way the other company was doing it. "I said: 'Well then, here's the thing. If we're going to run with them, we're going to have to work harder and do it the right way.' We did, and we ended up being successful."

Larry believes that being able to call on God for assistance in such difficult times is important. "I think prayer is talking to God. I can talk to God while I'm driving down the road, and sometimes I do. Sometimes God and I don't agree on everything. I get a little put out with God at times. I'm sure God gets put out with me at times too."

One of the keys to connecting with God, Larry says, is to "get off to the side, get away, get out of the flow, sit down someplace that's quiet, and slow it all down." When one has to make decisions and wants guidance from God, Larry says: "Think it out. Where are you going and what do you want? What are the important things?"

Over the years, Larry has come to realize that his worries as a young man were not so important. "I've got boxes of plaques in my basement. Back then [when I was young], they were so important. Now they're just pieces of wood. Sometimes it's a sign of weakness that someone has to dangle a piece of polished wood in front of you to get you to perform at the level God knows you can reach."

Larry does not claim to ever have been perfect, but he says his religion has taught him that God is forgiving. "I really believe that one of these days I'm going to be in heaven. I believe strongly that there is eternal happiness" he says.

Today, Larry is retired and works part-time. He enjoys volunteering and taking Communion to patients at the local hospital. "If I can make patients laugh a little bit and relieve their minds for a few minutes, if I can help distract them from a bad situation for just a little bit, I feel like I'm helping them. God has given me an opportunity to help people."

When Larry is a server at Mass, it is a different experience than when he was a child. Today, he says, "I feel an inner peace; I feel a closeness with God."

Larry encourages teenagers to get active in their parishes. "They have so many younger kids looking up to them. Once you start helping people, you feel so much better about yourself that you help yourself more than you do others."

4

Jesus calls us to follow him as a community

The Catholic Church follows the examples of Jesus and his disciples by creating a community of believers who worship and share their faith. From their connections to one another, many Catholics draw nourishment and experience love.

kristen day

Kristen says of her Catholic faith: "The commitment I made five years ago [when I converted] was to a new way of life. For me, every week, that commitment gives me new energy and reinforces my conviction that I'm doing the right thing. It keeps me on the right path." For Kristen, the energy comes from "being with all these people that feel the same way I do."

Kristen Day,
Executive Director, Democrats for Life

When Kristen Day began dating the man who would later become her husband, she decided to go to Mass with him. Although she had grown up Presbyterian, Kristen recalls, "I felt some sort of pull to the Catholic Church, so we went together."

That pull continued after they were married. Several years later, in 2001, Kristen decided she wanted to become Catholic. "We were going through a rough patch, trying to come together as a family. I felt that our faith and our going to church together brought us close, so I decided I was going to convert. My husband never asked me to [convert]. He didn't even expect me to. But he was so supportive and he sponsored me. Going through that experience together and feeling closer to God too were such wonderful things for my family and me."

Around that same time, many other things began to change in Kristen's life. She had been working as chief of staff for a congressman in Washington, D.C., sometimes dedicating sixty to seventy hours a week to her job. "I was frequently leaving home at 6:00 a.m. and not getting home until midnight," Kristen says. When she found out she was pregnant, she did not want to work the long hours any more.

> "My faith plays an important role in the job I've been doing. I feel as though my job is also my vocation."

Kristen had been working with a group of pro-life Democrats who wanted to form a new organization. "They offered me a job, and I was thrilled with the opportunity," she says. Kristen became the director of Democrats for Life, a national organization.

Democrats for Life has become one of the communities in which she puts her faith to work and from which she draws energy for her life as a Catholic. "My faith plays an important role in the job I've been doing," Kristen says. "I feel as though my job is also my vocation."

> "The social justice teachings of the Church are important to me. I think we need to renew our commitment to them, and not only the ones that pertain to pro-life issues."

"The social justice teachings of the Church are important to me. I think we need to renew our commitment to them, and not only the ones that pertain to pro-life issues."

Although Kristen's work is done within a community of faith, she finds that the faith community is important to her in other places as well. She says that one thing she treasures about her Catholic faith is "the sense of community and the sense of helping others. You see that as a Catholic, it's part of your life. It's a given that you help others."

Kristen's husband is involved with the Knights of Columbus, an organization that helps raise money for disabled children. She thinks it is rewarding to be part of a community in which one is expected to serve others.

Kristen's family community now includes her husband and two children. About the children she says, "I'm raising them with the value of helping others."

Kristen has found that being part of the Catholic community gives her comfort. Shortly after she came into the Church, she says, "I was going into the hospital and I had to write down my religion [on the admittance form]. I think that was the first time I had written down that I was Catholic. I felt such a sense of safety that I was going to be taken care of if anything happened to me. When I wrote it down, I felt as if everything was going to be okay."

Kristen Day promotes a pro-life world. She points out that her efforts are not only aimed at ending abortion. "As Catholics we have to expand the definition of what it is to be pro-life," she says. "I went to a briefing last week on Darfur (in Sudan) and the genocide that is going on there. We can't ignore the other aspects of life by focusing only on abortion. I'm committed to ending abortion because [I believe] it is killing, but I think we also need to expand the definition of what we look at as 'life.'"

bishop william houck

Bishop William Houck has lived in a Catholic community all his life. He grew up in Mobile, Alabama. His family was part of a Catholic environment that "was very supportive and provided a sense of security, a kind of joy. Everybody in the family was Catholic. It was always a joyful thing to be a Catholic."

Bishop William Houck,
President, Catholic Extension Society

When Bishop Houck was young, in grade school, he thought about becoming a priest. He felt comfortable around the church, liked being an altar server, and helped the nuns at the convent. "I began in those days to think that maybe God was calling me to the priesthood," he says. He liked the respect with which people treated priests and the idea of serving others.

Bishop Houck's faith continued to be important to him, especially when he received the sacraments of the Church, including Communion, Confirmation, and Ordination, and, years later, the Anointing of the Sick.

Bishop Houck realizes that the Church as an institution and Catholics as individuals have not always been paragons of virtue, as in the civil rights era of the 1960s. He says, however: "I do feel the Catholic Church has taken a stand and continues to take a stand on issues that are critical in life for us, and for society, and for the country, and for the world. That's when I'm proud of the Church, even when we suffer for taking a stand. For example, Catholics are concerned about the dignity of human life from conception to natural death; there's no question in society today where the Church stands on this issue."

"I do feel the Catholic Church has taken a stand and continues to take a stand on issues that are critical in life for us, and for society, and for the country, and for the world."

When a Catholic lives the faith, Bishop Houck notes, he or she is not living it alone. "Jesus didn't call us to follow him as rugged individualists, just me and Jesus. He called all of us to follow him as a community of people who care about one another and who together care about bringing Jesus and his message, his goodness, his forgiveness, his justice, and his service to other people."

> "I truly believe that it is good for us all to realize that we are—and each of these words is important—a Eucharistic, worshiping community of faith and love." That community, Bishop Houck says, "ties me together with other people who have similar goals in life."

Bishop Houck treasures "the community of faith and love that we have as Catholics, built around the center of faith in the Holy Eucharist. We have the real presence of Jesus in our community. I truly believe that it is good for us all to realize that we are—and each of these words is important—a Eucharistic, worshiping community of faith and love." That community, Bishop Houck says, "ties me together with other people who have similar goals in life."

He talks about how Jesus ultimately asked people to do more than just love one's neighbor as oneself. "I like to think that Jesus raised the bar on this matter of loving," Bishop Houck says. He points to the Last Supper, where Jesus gave his disciples a new commandment to love others as he loved them.

"Like every family, we [the Catholic Church] have our faults at times, we have our failures, we have our little spats; but we're still family. I love the Church and I will always love the Church," he says. "We're all on a journey of faith. Hopefully we're all trying to deepen our friendship, our intimate relationship with Jesus Christ. That is the thing that excites me and keeps me going."

It is not always easy. "I admit that in my life I have had to struggle as much as anybody else. In an active life, when you have responsibilities, it can be hard to be sure you give some priority to prayer. I have to keep struggling with that."

As a priest, he is able to celebrate Mass daily and he puts his faith to work in the way he relates to people. Bishop Houck asks others to pray for him. Prayers tie people together with the Universal Church, which is another thing Bishop Houck likes about being Catholic. "We are united together in the basic matters of faith, Catholic life, and the Eucharist," Bishop Houck says. "What a great treasure we have in our Catholic faith and what a gift it is to us. It is a gift that we disciples of Jesus are called not only to live but to share."

Bishop William Houck points out that Jesus said, "Go therefore and make disciples of all nations" (Matthew 28:19). "We're not a local, corner community that's gathered together without any connection with the rest of the world," he says. "Although we primarily experience our faith on the parish level, we also gather as a diocese and a worldwide Church."

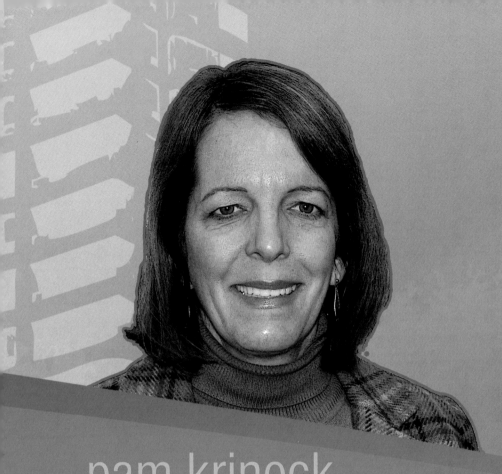

pam krinock

Pam Krinock married her Catholic husband in 1977. They attended his Catholic parish and her Lutheran church for nine years. When their daughter was born, Pam decided to take classes on the Catholic faith. "I wasn't buying too many of the piety customs, such as the saints or the veneration of the cross. It felt very foreign to me," she remembers. Then Pam and her husband went to a wedding at a Catholic Church with more modern architecture and fewer statues. Pam liked the priest's homily and the choir's music.

Pam Krinock, Director, Jesuit Volunteer Corps South

It was a small parish, so people noticed when someone new came into the church. The community made Pam and her husband feel welcome. Pam suggested to her husband that they start going to Mass there. "It was really a neat community, where parishioners made the bread for the Eucharist. They offered a Children's Church during the liturgy of the word and they asked me to be part of planning it, even though I wasn't Catholic," Pam says.

Many things began to draw Pam to the Catholic Church. "What was most appealing was the invitation to be involved. I started a spiritual exploration and found out there's not only one tradition in the Church but also a practice of personal prayer, such as Ignatian prayer. All of that made sense to me." Pam decided to learn more, and in 1988, she became a Catholic. Pam went on to study theology.

> Many things began to draw Pam to the Catholic Church. "What was most appealing was the invitation to be involved. I started a spiritual exploration."

Some of the things Pam has learned about the Church have not been easy to grasp. The Church's approach to sexual abuse problems has been one difficult issue. Another has been the ordination of women. "The Church is not open to women in ordained ministry," Pam says. That has been troubling to her because at one time, she felt called to be a leader in the Church. She has the necessary education and keeps a priest's stole hanging on the back of her office door so she will be ready if women's ordination is ever approved. "I won't be protesting or disrupting ordinations. But in order to maintain my integrity, I had to have a personal conversation with someone about [this issue]."

Pam approached the bishop in her diocese and asked for an appointment with him. He ignored her request and outlined his arguments against women's ordination in a letter. Next she tried the auxiliary bishop. She asked him if she could be accepted as a candidate for the deaconate. The bishop told her that even if he wanted to say yes, he could not. "So I asked him if he would listen to my story," she says. She remembers feeling like the woman in the Bible who asked Jesus to cure her daughter even though she had no reason to think he would. Jesus replied that because of her faith, he would do it.

> "I like the fact that my faith provides me with a spirituality that helps me integrate all parts of life, including work and family."

The bishop could not accept Pam for ordination, but he did listen. "I asked for advice about how to live with the pain this issue causes me," she says. "He was silent for a few minutes. That was a good response because if he had said something right away, I would have thought he was just using platitudes."

In the end, he did not have an answer for her, but Pam felt satisfied that she had told her story. She asked him to share it at an upcoming meeting where all the bishops in the country would be discussing a pastoral letter on women's roles in the Church. Pam says: "I guess that's where I just put things in God's hands. Having done that was the first step for me in living with the pain and spiritual discouragement."

Pam recognizes that the faith has brought joy to her daily life, especially through the sacraments. "Symbols such as fire, oil, wheat, and bread are the things that help me tie into daily life," she says. "The notion of sacraments and God coming to us through ordinary people in everyday life helps me."

She sees God everywhere and finds her faith especially important in her family life. Her two children, she says, are sometimes her teachers. Pam remembers a time when her husband was away in Kuwait for a year and she felt sad and lonely. She went to Mass with her children. One Sunday, before she received the Eucharist, she listened to the words she was reciting with the congregation: "Lord, I am not worthy to receive you, but only say the word and I shall be healed" (*Sacramentary,* p. 564.) After Communion, her son leaned over and asked if she was feeling better. She said no, so he persisted, "Weren't you healed?" Pam realizes, "The words at the Mass became something to believe, not just something rote."

Pam says: "I like the fact that my faith provides me with a spirituality that helps me integrate all parts of life, including work and family. And it helps me find a community of people with whom I want to be associated."

Pam's faith is important in her job with the Jesuit Volunteer Corps. The corps creates opportunities for volunteers to work with community- and church-based agencies, serving people who have AIDS, at-risk youths, immigrants, and others in need. "We take [our volunteers] out of their comfort zone and place them with those who have a different view of the world. I think of that and realize it would be hard to build the Kingdom of God on my own. Instead of just me, it's also these fifty or more people who are going into the region every year."

Pam Krinock likes the spirituality developed by Saint Ignatius of Loyola. The teachings of Jesus are the basis for this spirituality, which emphasizes reflection and prayer. It leads Pam to ask herself: "Where is God being revealed to me today? What will I do for Christ? Sometimes I substitute the names of people because we see Christ in all people. So I might put in the name of my daughter, or a homeless person I pass, or someone with whom I need to reconcile. That's kind of a concrete way to keep my faith real and not just theoretical."

sr. katarina schuth

For Sr. Katarina Schuth, faith has long been about connecting with people in all aspects of life. She grew up in a Catholic family on a farm along the Mississippi River. When Katarina was a child, the family regularly attended Mass and said the rosary together during special times. She cherishes the memory of the way her parents taught their children about faith. "It was a faith that was to be practiced in the ways we interacted with people—family and neighbors, friends and strangers—as well as in doing good works."

Sr. Katarina Schuth, College Professor, Saint Paul Seminary School of Divinity, University of Saint Thomas

As a Franciscan sister, Katarina looks back on a retreat she attended in high school that might have been the root of her vocation. The Jesuits who led the conference encouraged quiet and listening for God's voice during prayer. "The retreat leader asked us to reflect on lines from a reading of Psalm 23, the Lord is my Shepherd," she says. The notion that God could speak to people, that each person is of infinite value, was important. Katarina says, "I remember experiencing something of God's presence, and I thought, this is so wonderful that it's really worth trying to do again."

When she attended college, Katarina took it for granted that she would continue to practice her faith. "It reminds me of the time when Jesus said to Peter, 'are you going to leave me too?' Peter said, 'Lord, where would I go?' I knew there was no other place for me to go to keep my faith alive."

> "I have a determination each day to meet and greet people in a way that will make them feel better because they have met me."

Katarina has continued to draw on prayer, whether formal, personal, or communal, as a source of strength in her daily life. Prayer helps her live each day, keeping others in mind. "I have a determination each day to meet and greet people in a way that will make them feel better because they have met me. I want to ask God for what they might need or be thinking about or be worrying about or be involved in at this time in their lives."

She believes it is especially valuable in her relationships with students. She tries to get to know each one personally. "When I learn about some of their family situations and about their goals and aspirations in life, I have a more positive and more complete view of them and recognize the struggles many of them are having."

Time at Mass is also important to Katarina. "I treasure the sense of coming together to pray and the notion that when you're with other people who believe in and identify with some of the same things you do as being important in their lives, that is something that is really very valuable," she says. "It provides a sense of belonging, of being there with others who are looking for the same thing: meaning in their lives. We're all looking for a way to answer some of the deepest questions about life and death."

"Being Catholic is such a complete life experience. There's a fullness about it," she says. "It starts with our relationship with God and the spiritual dimension that is so central and given deeper meaning through the sacraments."

> "Being Catholic is such a complete life experience. There's a fullness about it."

Katarina finds that Catholic social teaching contains a call to reach out. "These teachings are a guide to our external expression of faith, a reaching out beyond the familiar to those in need. The teachings of the Church regarding our care for others are so clear and so insistent. We have a responsibility to respect life at every stage and in all forms, to live in peace, to express our love for people everywhere. It means we have to work for economic and social justice in all aspects of our society, to care for the earth. These are some of the ways the teachings of the Church lead us to work for a better world."

One concrete way Katarina tries to fulfill this responsibility is through her involvement with the Catholic Common Ground Initiative. Cardinal Joseph Bernardin began this initiative in 1992 to encourage people to engage in dialogue with one another, listen to the hopes and dreams of others, and respect others' ways of understanding God in their lives. Cardinal Bernardin's efforts have continued beyond his death. Katarina remains involved in working toward peace and reconciliation among many different church groups.

She remembers speaking at a gathering of parish men's associations about the Catholic Common Ground efforts several years ago. One man said he did not think people should be discussing topics that might involve church regulations, but rather, should just uphold them. Katarina did her best to explain why it is necessary for people to talk about their faith. It did not help; afterward, the man approached her, still angry.

"I knew there was no answer that would satisfy him, so I prayed to the Holy Spirit for inspiration—silently, of course. At one point, when he paused, I put my hand on his shoulder and said, 'God must love you very much.' He was shocked and said, 'Why are you saying that?' I responded, 'Well, I can tell by your concerns that you care a lot about the Church and you want things to be done correctly and you care that the Church will prosper."

She continued by recounting the story of the disciples after the Resurrection. They were afraid. When Jesus arrived to comfort them, he said, "Peace be with you!" Katarina said to the man, "That's my wish for you: that peace be with you."

"At that, the man suddenly burst into tears. It was at that moment I realized that sometimes when we don't know what to say, God's words come to us and God's intervention brings healing. It seemed to be a great moment of grace. I think that having a sense of trust that God will inspire us if we are attuned to God's presence in our lives is essential."

Sr. Katarina Schuth says that young people can deepen their prayer life "by practice and by trying different methods of prayer that people suggest to them." She recommends reading a Scripture passage and choosing one of the characters in the passage. Then one can try to see how God is acting in that person. "What would it be like to be that person in the story? How is God working in that person's life? in my life?"

5

the Eucharist puts God in our midst

Although there are many things Catholics like about their Church, it is the Eucharist, the real presence of Jesus, that ultimately draws them to Catholicism.

bob lefnesky

Bob grew up in a Catholic family with parents who were deeply involved in the Church. He knew God was important but thought of religion more as something he would "do" when he was older and had his own family. That view changed when his mother suggested he attend a retreat. Bob did not want to go, but because he would get a day off from school if he went, he said yes.

Bob Lefnesky, also known as Righteous B, Professional Rapper

He remembers hanging out in the back of the room at the retreat and not paying much attention to what was going on. A guy in the front of the room was talking about God's love—not a new topic to Bob. But the speaker was expressing himself with a passion Bob had not heard before. The speaker later approached Bob and said, "I think God wants to do something in your life."

Bob considered the speaker's words to him. He walked on the beach and prayed, asking God to make himself as real to Bob as God was to the speaker. "That was the beginning of falling in love with God," Bob remembers. After that, practicing his faith was not merely optional or one little aspect of his life; it was a way of living, a part of everything he did. That experience helped Bob claim his Catholic faith as his own. It was not just something his parents had taught him; it was something he had chosen for himself.

Although Bob's faith has been especially important to him during challenging times in his life, it has also been an integral part of his everyday life. "It's life-giving on a daily basis. It's foundational," he says. One of his favorite Bible verses is John 10:10: "I came that they may have life and have it abundantly."

"I'm alive with the sacraments of the Church, especially the Eucharist," Bob says. "It's one thing for Christ to die for us but another for him to be here every day for us.

> "It's one thing for Christ to die for us but another for him to be here every day for us. It constantly blows my mind. It's a wild mystery."

It constantly blows my mind. It's a wild mystery." Bob finds the depth of the gift of the Eucharist spelled out in John, chapter 6.

Understanding that Jesus is truly present in the Eucharist can lead people to do things in their lives that they never expected to. "My vocation is first to be a lover of God. We all wear lots of hats and have many duties, but that's what I do. I do it by taking time to pray, participating in the sacraments, and reading the Scriptures," Bob says.

Bob also does it through his work as a musician and by being a husband and father. In 2005, he and his wife asked for God's guidance when they considered starting a nonprofit organization for inner-city children in Ohio. They decided to go ahead with it. "God wanted us to take a step in faith," Bob says. Bob did not know what would happen if he left his youth ministry job to be a full-time musician. Taking the risk has paid off. "[My wife and I] want to say yes to whatever it is God asks of us. Since we made this change, we've been at the best place ever as a family, spiritually and financially."

> "I can be in Europe, Alaska, or New Jersey and when I enter a Catholic Church, [I feel as if] I'm home."

Because Bob's work takes him to various places, he experiences the diverse beauty of the Church. "One of the greatest treasures is the Body of Christ, the community," he says. "I can be in Europe, Alaska, or New Jersey and when I enter a Catholic Church, [I feel as if] I'm home." In this universal Church, Bob sees beauty, diversity, and unity. "I see the different corners of the Church and I know that my story is part of a bigger whole."

The bigger whole is based on a history of ritual that Bob sees as one of the greatest beauties of the Church. "We can be a part of it," Bob says. "We can be a chain in that ritual. We can live out our faith."

Bob Lefnesky sees the Eucharist as filling a basic human need for closeness. When he sees how people use e-mail, text messaging, cell phones, and other forms of communication, "it all speaks of this starving desire for intimacy. The Eucharist is Christ reaching out to meet our need for intimacy. The infinite is also the intimate. We can let that intimacy transform our hearts."

susan sucher

Susan Sucher grew up in an Assemblies of God church and later attended a Baptist church. When she began dating a Catholic man who attended Mass every Sunday, she felt obligated to learn about the Catholic faith, even though she had heard negative things about it during her youth. When she began to ask questions, she realized that some of the things she had heard were not true.

Susan Sucher, Mother and Teacher

"I laid out my concerns right away," she remembers. The first concern was that she did not believe Mary was God. The deacon assured her that Catholics did not believe Mary was God, either. Susan's understanding of the Church began to grow.

Another Church teaching she disagreed with was birth control. "I thought it was a bunch of celibate men telling women what to do," she remembers. "The more I looked into it, the more I realized that it's about husband and wife being together as a unit, with nothing separating them. That was respecting my dignity."

Understanding led Susan to an appreciation of the Church's teachings about women, some of which she found in the writings of Pope John Paul II. "We're not objects. We are designed to be life-giving. I'm all right the way I am made by nature.

"I started looking into all my questions. I read the *Catechism* and the encyclicals. It all made sense." Susan says her study of the faith "turned into a love for the Church because it was the only time I have ever found that it's all laid out and it doesn't change." In Protestant churches, she explains, one pastor might have a different interpretation of the Bible than another pastor.

> "I started looking into all my questions. I read the *Catechism* and the encyclicals. It all made sense."

Something stronger also drew Susan to the Church. She believed that because of the Last Supper, Communion was important. As she studied Catholicism, she learned about the real presence of Jesus in the Eucharist. "That is what blows me away every time I think about it. Jesus humbles himself to be with us."

After the 9-11 tragedy, Susan desired the real presence of Christ. "That's something other churches don't even claim to have," she says. "Any time I want to, I can go to the Church to be with Christ. It's a beautiful, intimate thing."

"The [Eucharist] gives me strength. I feel sorry for those who don't have it," she says. "For me, it's what gets me through."

A big part of Susan's understanding of the Eucharist came from reading John, chapter 6, and listening to Catholic teachings about the Eucharist. The idea of the real presence did not make sense to her at first, but after hearing explanations of it, she began to understand that Jesus was not speaking symbolically or metaphorically. "He didn't turn around and say, 'Just joking.' He kept saying that really difficult thing," she says, referring to his directive to "Eat my body and drink my blood."

"How phenomenally outrageous is that? Either it's crazy or it's true. If I'm going to be a Bible-believing person, I have to believe it's true."

Susan appreciates the two thousand years of beauty, tradition, and prayer and the lives of the saints she finds in the Church. "By reading, by knowing about the lives of the saints, and by practicing some of the traditions such as praying the rosary, I am drawing on the wealth and wisdom of all those hundreds of years."

> "The [Eucharist] gives me strength. I feel sorry for those who don't have it. For me, it's what gets me through."

The many spiritualities of the Church, such as the Carmelites, Franciscans, and Benedictines, provide tools for all sorts of people to learn to live their lives as Catholics.

Susan feels that her ministry at this stage in her life is taking care of her children. When she married, she had two children; now she has two more. She left her career as an actuary to care for her children and homeschool them. Whether Susan is changing a diaper or teaching geography, "I make it a prayer, something I can offer to God."

When she is able, Susan attends Mass on weekdays. She chooses to be Catholic now because of the Eucharist. "That's why I keep coming back. It's the source and the summit."

Susan Sucher appreciates Catholic teachings about God's mercy. As she was growing up, attending a church in another denomination, she feared that when the rapture came, she could be left behind because of one small sin. She does not fear this anymore. "God is not some sort of heavenly tally maker. I feel God's mercy more in the Catholic Church. I see God more as a loving father."

sue borders

As a teen, Sue considered becoming a missionary sister. Her mother said no. "My mother said that when I was eighteen, if I still wanted to do that, fine. But she was not going to let me leave at thirteen. She was very wise."

Sue Borders, Retired Speech Therapist

Sue did not become a missionary. She married, had children, and worked as a speech therapist. Today she still feels drawn to the Mass and recognizes how the Church has always been a part of her life. Like Sue, the Church has evolved. Sue has examined issues within the Church and knows it is not perfect, but she still feels proud to be a Catholic.

One strong reason for that is the Eucharist. "I treasure the relationship with Jesus that I have through the Eucharist," Sue says. "It's the pivotal point of any Mass or liturgy. It's such a beautiful command to do as Jesus does. He gives up his body and blood and calls us into the mystery of salvation. I feel a comfort there. I feel so privileged to believe in the Eucharist and not just receive Jesus but be received by Jesus in Communion. It's a mutual love affair."

> "I treasure the relationship with Jesus that I have through the Eucharist." It's the pivotal point of any Mass or liturgy."

Through the Eucharist, Sue says, "we are being reunited with the Body of Christ that tries to keep serving and loving God and keep from sinning."

She also loves the fact that no matter where she is, the Eucharist is the most joyful part of the Mass. "It's awesome to know that I'm part of something that is repeated hundreds of thousands of times throughout the world."

Sue believes that all the sacraments "are like windows into the soul." Reconciliation, she says, is challenging but also comforting. "When the sacrament of Penance and Reconciliation is occurring, Jesus is there."

There are always times in life when the hatred and sadness in the world invade one's thoughts to make things difficult. When Sue was in her late thirties and early forties, her father was ill with cancer. While she was caring for him, she was also coping with her mother's Alzheimer's disease. Her twin sister went through a difficult divorce. Her children were "lippy" teenagers. Workers at her husband's place of employment went on strike; because of the strike, the Borders family sometimes found nails on their driveway. "Everywhere I turned, I felt as if I found chaos," she says. "It was a time when I felt overburdened and overwhelmed." She realized that the cross is part of everyone's life. Although she was angry with God, she could still pray and talk with God.

> "My spirit grew when I realized I was dependent on God in many ways. That was a very, very difficult time in my life, but my faith in God and my relationship with God sustained me."

"My spirit grew when I realized I was dependent on God in many ways," she says. "That was a very, very difficult time in my life, but my faith in God and my relationship with God sustained me."

Sue recognized that at times, people have to make a conscious decision not to live in worry. She decided: "I'm going to live in hope. I'm going to trust that Jesus died and suffered. I too can suffer, but that doesn't mean God does not love me. Ultimately, God is there to save me from all this."

While Sue was dealing with all of these issues, someone nominated her for parish pastoral council. Her first instinct was to say no, that she did not have time to be on the council. But she decided to say yes. "It turned out to be one bright spot in the hard times. In fact, I would say I had a feeling of reconversion, in a sense, at that point."

These days life is calmer. Sue prays every morning. She tries to attend Mass daily. She has retired from her job as a speech therapist, so she helps with things at the parish.

"I try to live out what God's will is for me," Sue says. "I don't know what that is exactly, but I take it day by day. I figure that whatever situation or event I find myself in, that's where I have an opportunity to be a faith witness or not."

Sue Borders hopes she is an example of faith for her children and grandchildren. "I try to make them aware that God is there. I tell them to listen to see if they can live out what God's will is for them."

6

asking questions leads to life changes

Many people struggle to make sense of teachings about the Church and faith. They have asked questions and gotten answers. This process has challenged them to take paths in their lives that might have at one time seemed unthinkable.

anne rice

Anne Rice does not think that losing one's faith during one's college years, as she did, is uncommon. "I think many, many, many college kids go through this. I grew up in a sheltered, detailed, rich world in which religion was a reality. Then I went out into a different environment and was exposed to different influences. It was hard to figure it all out."

Anne Rice, Bestselling Author

"I saw a whole other world that was functioning without the Catholic faith and without the kind of religious behavior I was brought up to believe was necessary for a good life. And yet the people in this other world were good people," she remembers. "I simply could not believe what I had been brought up to believe. It didn't square with what I saw."

The years Anne spent away from the Church were very different from her childhood years in an Irish-German Catholic parish in New Orleans. She describes the New Orleans of her youth as old-fashioned, with its beautiful, old-style architecture. Her family life revolved around the parish.

"We sort of lived and breathed our Catholic faith. It was saturation. It was a wonderful world. We had a strong sense of community and a very, very, very strong sense of the meaning of life and our place in the universe. It was really quite wonderful."

> When she was fourteen years old, Anne's life began to change. Her mother died, and her father moved the family to Texas. It was like moving to another country. . . .

When she was fourteen years old, Anne's life began to change. Her mother died, and her father moved the family to Texas. It was like moving to another country for a girl whose family had owned a television set for only a year. "We didn't even get a TV until I was thirteen, because my family was against it. We were the sort of Catholics who distrusted anything modern, anything secular, anything imperialistic."

In the suburbs of Dallas, Anne met very few Catholics. When she left home at eighteen to attend college, she met even fewer. She studied philosophy, tested her ideas, and met many people who were good but did not attend church. In this atmosphere, she became an atheist. "I felt that we don't know if God exists and we may be in a world without God. That means we have to be really good because we are the only ones who have a conscience in this world. There is no overriding consciousness running everything. Of course, I didn't realize that this is written about right there in the Gospel of Matthew: 'Be perfect, therefore, as your heavenly father is perfect' (5:48). I didn't think of it that way."

Part of her confusion came from being thrown into a Protestant world that she did not understand. Growing up as a Catholic, she says, there were ways you "paid your dues," such as getting up early for Mass and fasting before Communion. "You worked at it."

> Anne saw that many changes had taken place in the Church, and she asked questions. She did not understand everything about how the Church had evolved.

"It wasn't enough to simply mow your grass and say 'I've taken Jesus as my Savior' and then go watch the football game. That's kind of what I saw around me." Anne now knows that she did not understand Protestantism.

After living on the West Coast for thirty years, Anne and her husband moved to New Orleans. She reconnected with her cousins, who were very religious. "It was interesting to be around them and see how seriously they took their faith and how they had adjusted to the modern world."

Anne saw that many changes had taken place in the Church, and she asked questions. She did not understand everything about how the Church had evolved.

For example, she feared that she had been excommunicated because she had married outside the Church. She did not understand the Church's view of homosexuality or how it aligned with what she thought it should be.

Anne began questioning friends. She asked one particularly devout man, "'How do I go back to a Church that says my gay son is going to hell?' I remember he shrugged his shoulders and said, 'Our God is an all-merciful God.'"

"I couldn't get that out of my mind. I think that finally I realized that of course God will work out these theological, social questions. I don't have to work them out," she says. "A God who can make the world can do anything. I think I glimpsed what it means to trust in God."

> "A God who can make the world can do anything. I think I glimpsed what it means to trust in God."

Even though she did not know all the answers, Anne went to Church and had a wonderful experience celebrating the sacrament of Penance and Reconciliation. She learned that she had not been excommunicated. She did need to get married in the Church. Her husband agreed to a Catholic wedding, and the couple married in Anne's childhood parish.

Being in that parish again reminded Anne of her childhood. "When I was a child and I heard that my mother had died, I walked over to Church. I was in a state of shock; I could hardly function. I walked up the aisle to the altar of Our Mother of Perpetual Help and talked to her. I told her, 'My mother is dead. It's awful. Our lives are going to be completely different, and I don't know what's going to happen.' I remember talking to her and turning to her instinctively."

Anne found herself at the same altar forty years later, once again a member of the Catholic faith. She was preparing to move out of New Orleans. "I caught myself saying, 'I haven't knelt before you since that first time. I'm coming now again,'"

Anne says. Although her separation from the Church had left her feeling as though she had an open wound in the years she had been away, she realized, "that by coming back to New Orleans, by going back to the Church, I had stopped the bleeding. God had stopped it."

Anne treasures her devotion to Mary, and says, "I also like the way that we have saints for all minds, that we have a huge body of pondering and studying that can include great diversity. Our Church is not really a monolith; it's a great compendium of meditations and ideas and all different ways of moving closer to the Lord. There's something for everyone in that; there are so many ways to approach our Lord."

Anne says one of her biggest challenges is loving unconditionally. Sometimes she fails. In 2005, after Hurricane Katrina, she wrote an editorial for the *New York Times* about the greatness of New Orleans. It was a mostly positive piece, except for the section on her belief that the nation had turned its back on the city. "I was basing [my assessment] on what I saw on television about how people were turning away from one another during the storm, when the city was being flooded."

> Another key to Anne's Catholicism is believing that Christ is truly present on the altar during Mass. "That is something I feel deeply about as a Catholic."

She received complimentary e-mail messages about the piece but also some critical messages. At first, she snapped back at the critics. Then she realized "that If I believe what I say I believe, I have to be loving to these people. No matter what they say to me, I have to do this. I actually wrote to one woman and said 'I apologize to you.'"

"Going to Mass every week, that's easy. Saying the rosary, that's a pleasure. Contributing to the Church, that's no problem," Anne says. Going beyond that can be difficult.

Another key to Anne's Catholicism is believing that Christ is truly present on the altar during Mass. "That is something I feel deeply about as a Catholic," she says. "You're not going to find a better love story anywhere than the one about Christ coming, and becoming one of us, and dying, and bringing us to him. It doesn't get any better than that."

Anne Rice says that even after she returned to the Church, "there was still a long way to go before I had committed my work to Christ. I made the commitment in 2002 that I wouldn't write anything that wasn't for him. That was another point of conversion, you could say, where I felt as though I had made a full commitment to him. I said, 'Thy will be done.'" In 2005, she published the first novel in a trilogy based on the life of Christ, *Christ the Lord: Out of Egypt* (Knopf).

martina derose

Martina DeRose was baptized Catholic as an infant
but did not go to church because her mother was ill and unable
to attend. She grew up attending an evangelical Christian church with
her grandmother. As a teenager, Martina was devoted to appearance.
She studied to be a hairdresser, went to fashion shows, and modeled for
hairstyle books. She also met her husband when she was working as a
hairstylist.

Martina DeRose, Mother and Teacher

When she married, Martina says she was self-centered. "It had to be my way or no way, in picking out stuff for the house, having kids." Even when she did have children, she thought: "They're not going to interrupt my space. I'm not going to get up with them." Around her she saw women who had children but still managed to go out with friends and have a good time. She thought her life would be the same as theirs.

Then she started exploring her faith. Martina had drifted away from church. But her husband had been raised Catholic, so they attended Mass together. Even though Martina had been baptized Catholic, she knew nothing about the Church. She asked her husband about it, but his typical reply was "I don't know. The nuns said we had to."

With the struggles and challenges that marriage and parenthood presented, Martina says: "I figured I had to have something to hold onto. Bible verses and memorization weren't going to do it for me. I decided I needed to go to the Rite of Christian Initiation of Adults (RCIA). My husband and I have both learned a lot since then."

During the RCIA, Martina got answers to her questions. She learned why Catholics make the sign of the cross on the heart, lips, and forehead and when they do it. She learned that this action symbolizes the Gospel's staying in her heart, on her lips, and in her mind all day.

"Bible verses and memorization weren't going to do it for me. I decided I needed to go to the Rite of Christian Initiation of Adults (RCIA)."

She wanted to know why Catholics go to confession. "I went once or twice a year, but I didn't understand why. Years went by, and slowly it started to come together. Eventually, I came to the realization that I'm not perfect and I have a lot of faults. I felt that I needed to take myself out of everything instead of being so selfish and stubborn and to be more giving to my family. Confession helped me with that." Celebrating the sacrament of Penance and Reconciliation, Martina says, "makes me feel right, and every time I go it feels more right for me. It helps me remember that I'm just a little speck and the whole world doesn't revolve around me."

After delving more deeply into her faith, Martina came upon another revelation. "By coming to know my faith, I realized that I can't learn things and then just jot them down in a notebook. I have to live my faith. That was the big 'Oh! Now I get it!' It's supposed to come out in my actions all day, every day, in my thoughts and in everything I do. Slowly, I started to take myself out of it; I was compelled to be more giving."

> "By coming to know my faith, I realized that I can't learn things and then just jot them down in a notebook. I have to live my faith. That was the big 'Oh! Now I get it!'"

These days Martina puts her faith to work consistently as she raises and homeschools her six children. The family prays together daily and reads about the saint of the day. If they are not able to attend Mass, they read the Scriptures together. They also enjoy celebrating the seasons of the Church.

Some seasons and actions, such as Lent and making sacrifices, are more challenging than others. "Helping to hold one another to our promises is important." Martina says.

Fun activities, such as putting out shoes to celebrate the feast day of Saint Nicholas, "make me feel like a kid again. I get excited about those times."

"I would forget about those things if I weren't following the Church calendar. I would get so absorbed in the laundry, the dishes, and the schoolwork. Turning that next page in the [liturgical] calendar helps me to stay connected with the Church when I can't always be at Church during the week."

In the midst of everyday life, interruptions to the routine sometimes remind Martina of the importance of her faith. In 2005, when the family was remodeling a house and preparing to move, Martina's husband became ill. The doctors were not sure what was wrong with him. At some point, Martina remembered a prayer she had made for an increase of faith. It seemed apparent that God was answering her prayer by giving her challenges that required exactly that response. "Without my faith, I would have mentally crumbled."

"[I saw that experience as] God talking to us again, being right there with us, and letting us know he's always there with us. As hard as I think it was, we kept it together mentally because of our faith," Martina says. This experience, which ended with her husband's full recovery, taught her to remember always that God will give one the grace to bear the difficulties in life. "I didn't realize that before I had my faith."

Earlier in her life, Martina recalls, "I felt that I had been handed some sort of faith and I didn't hold onto it. I memorized all the books of the Bible and all these wonderful songs, but what was underneath it? Why? Why? The why wasn't there for me."

Today Martina treasures being Catholic. "It's my own journey, but I'm together with a community of people around the whole world."

To get through her busy days, Martina DeRose likes to reflect on a spiritual reading before her children wake up. She enjoys the homilies of Josemariá Escrivá and the writings of Saint Augustine. Some of the readings have taught her that "people struggled back then just like people struggle with their demons today. It's a full circle; we're all connected."

bernie choiniere

Bernie Choiniere was like a lot of Catholic kids. He went to church with his family on Sundays. He attended Catholic school for six years and learned from the nuns. He received the sacraments. "I was a regular young Catholic kid."

Bernie Choiniere,
Musician and Inspirational Speaker

When Bernie reached adolescence, he continued to go through the motions of attending Mass but carried doubts within himself. He pondered the possibility that God did not exist. When he started college, he stopped attending Church and had no prayer life. "I basically went down that darker road," Bernie remembers.

After graduating with a degree in music theatre, Bernie pursued a career on the stage for a while but became depressed and frustrated with his craft. He joined a rock band. He dabbled in drugs and used alcohol. "I was living a not-so-holy life."

During the day, Bernie worked at a store selling pianos. He was not happy with his life but was not doing anything to change it. One day his cousin came into the store to visit him. She was preparing for a trip to Medjugorje and shared some of the miracle stories she had heard about the place. God was not on Bernie's mind in those days, but when his cousin left the store, he began to ponder questions about God. He said to God, if you are real, make yourself known to me in a real way.

> "I basically went down that darker road. I was living a not-so-holy life."

Three days later, Bernie went to work. A man had been at the store and left him a book called *The Secret of the Rosary*, by Saint Louis de Montfort (Monfort Publications, 1954). He read it that afternoon. He was intrigued but not convinced.

When Bernie's cousin returned from her trip, she gave Bernie a rosary. Bernie began to pray one decade of the rosary a day. After three months, he decided that if he wanted to be closer to God, he should go to church. He listened and asked questions.

One day after Mass, Bernie got into his car to drive home and tried to continue praying the rosary. As he was driving, he looked into the sky and saw a cloud in the shape of a cross. It was the size of a stadium and filled the sky. "I was completely blown away," he remembers. "I was so filled with joy and peace."

The revelation was not complete, however. Bernie felt God guiding his thoughts back to when he had received Communion during Mass. Bernie felt God was giving him a sign that God is "truly present in the Eucharist." Everything Bernie had learned as a child began to seem real to him. "I felt as though God, in an instant, was giving me wisdom. My whole life had changed overnight." God was answering Bernie's prayer.

> Bernie felt God was giving him a sign that God is "truly present in the Eucharist."

Bernie began to change his lifestyle. His bandmates noticed it and made fun of him. It was a difficult time. Bernie knew he had to quit playing in the band. He feared that when he did, he might also lose the music store job because the store was connected with the band. When Bernie decided to resign, he played one last time, knowing it would be the last. That night, a piece of equipment fell on his foot, injuring it and causing it to swell. He knew he would have to see the doctor the next day, but before he did that, he wanted to resign from the band. As he was preparing to tell the other band members, he remembered he did not have his rosary with him, so he returned to his car to retrieve it. After he got it and went back inside, he realized his foot no longer hurt. He attributes this event, and others, to God's presence in his life.

Bernie eventually left the rock band to write and perform Catholic music. He began working in parishes and giving witness talks to young people. He has particularly focused on doubting-Thomas teens, young people who do not believe what they were taught as children.

Bernie does this work because he loves his faith and wants to be an extension of God's hands and words in the world. He embraces his faith publicly as he plays throughout New England and at national youth events. Bernie says his transformation does not mean he is no longer a sinner. It does mean he takes his doubts to God and finds comfort in his faith. "I think it's cool to be Catholic."

janet smith

Like many college students who were raised Catholic, Janet Smith sought a home outside the Church for a short while. During the 1960s, Janet wanted to become a radical, "to fight for human rights along with my generation," she remembers. "But before long, I decided that [many of my peers] didn't know much about reality."

Janet Smith, PhD,
College Professor, Sacred Heart Major Seminary

"They spoke of policemen as 'pigs,' but my grandfather was a policeman and he was no pig. They talked about identifying with the working class, but my family was working class and my peers had no idea what my family was all about."

In 1969, women came to the campus to talk with students about writing letters in favor of legalizing abortion. "I had never heard of abortion. I went to the library and read about it. I was shocked. I thought babies and pregnancy were great and couldn't believe that women would [choose abortion]."

Janet recalls that her research about abortion taught her two things: She learned when life begins and she learned the Catholic Church's teaching against abortion. She went to the meeting organized by the women who were in favor of abortion. "I asked them when they thought human life began. They told me to shut up and sit down. They said, 'We don't want your kind here.' I didn't know what they meant. Before long, I was going back to Church," Janet says. "I figured if the Church was right about abortion, it might be right about other things. I found the Church's teaching about contraception to be spectacularly true and so at odds with the culture that I was impressed with [the Church's] courage and perseverance."

> "I figured if the Church was right about abortion, it might be right about other things."

Making the choice to return to the Church did not make life easy for Janet. She enjoyed the company of intellectuals and loved exploring philosophy, but she found that many people she knew who also enjoyed those things were against religion, specifically Catholicism. Nevertheless, she continued searching for others who shared some of her beliefs and interests. When she went to Toronto to study for her PhD, she found them. She and her friends, who were wonderful Catholics, formed a Thomas Aquinas reading group, a pro-life group, a Vatican II reading group, and a Bible study group. "We also partied and went to plays and picnics and bookstores and lectures and concerts. It was a wonderful period of my life," Janet recalls.

> She believes that Catholics think deeply about important matters. "It is challenging because it may make us change and may make us unpopular," she says.

Janet stayed in the intellectual atmosphere, teaching at Notre Dame, the University of Dallas, and Sacred Heart Major Seminary.

One continuous theme throughout Janet's student days and career as a professor has been the pursuit of truth, a pursuit that is very much connected with her Catholicism. She acknowledges that speaking the truth is not always easy. She believes that Catholics think deeply about important matters. "It is challenging because it may make us change and may make us unpopular," she says. "I have had to change some of my behavior because of what the Church teaches, and I have lost a job and friends and been unpopular in various ways because of what the Church teaches. Of course, I have also made many friends because I embrace Church teachings."

"I think that truth seekers will find Christ and the Church and then get on their knees to ask for forgiveness and guidance and then soar and luxuriate in the graces and gifts that God sends. They weave in and out of confusion, bliss, misery, joy, love, stress, adventures, and epiphanies galore."

The epiphanies do not always happen with a loud bang. Janet has found that in trying to do God's will, it is important to take one step at a time. "We know when we are doing God's will, when we are not breaking the commandments, and when we are trying to learn and live by the Church's teaching," she says. "After that, we need to learn how to pray and spend time in prayer, especially before the Blessed Sacrament. We should begin each day with prayer and end each day with prayer and ask God to help us shape our choices during the day. Often people want to know the big plan God has for their lives, but that plan is worked out through a series of choices. People usually know what they are supposed to do today, tomorrow, and the day after that; that is about all we need to know."

"The Church has a fantastic intellectual tradition that helps us know the Truth. Knowing the Truth helps us know how to live." Janet had the example of her parents to follow in her faith life. She describes them as being virtuous people. The faith she inherited and then affirmed for herself, Janet says, "gives me a reason to live and helps me know how to live."

catholic social teaching gives me a home in the church

They participate in marches, vote to encourage change in society, and protest inhumane practices by purchasing certain goods and services. People who study Catholic social teachings may put their faith into action so that all people will be treated with the loving care that Jesus exhibited.

teresa capecchi

Teresa Capecchi has been to Guatemala and Palestine. She has protested the Iraq War in Washington, D.C., and fasted in solidarity with detainees at Guantanamo Bay. She has planned service trips that open the world to students. She did all of this before she was twenty years old. Why? Because she is Catholic.

Teresa Capecchi, College Student

"I am completely inspired by Jesus's message and way of life," Teresa says. "I think it's the ideal way to live: in the service of others. Catholicism in its essence promotes social justice in such a way that I can't help but continue to be Catholic."

Jesus, Teresa points out, helped any person who needed him, without making judgments. "He didn't think about society's views of different people. If people lived their lives in the same way he did, we would have the ideal world; if people lived for one another rather than for themselves."

Teresa was raised Catholic. She attended a Catholic high school in Minneapolis, and that is where she first learned about social justice. A religion teacher told her about Architects, Relationships, Knowledge: Journeys of Hope (ARK), an organization that arranges student exchanges in Guatemala, Palestine, and the United States. ARK exists to empower, unite, and help equip globally diverse youth to become architects of a culture of peace through building relationships, expanding knowledge, and constructing a new road map for peace. "I went to Guatemala and saw the need people had; I got a world view," Teresa says.

> "I went to Guatemala and saw the need people had; I got a world view. Before I traveled there, I hadn't thought about other places or about doing anything globally."

"Before I traveled there, I hadn't thought about other places or about doing anything globally. I realized how necessary it is for us to go out of our way to help others and to make changes when I saw the oppression in Guatemala and heard the stories of oppression in Palestine."

These experiences moved Teresa deeply. After returning home, she reflected on them for a long time before she figured out how to integrate what she had learned into her life. She sometimes shied away from talking about her experiences for fear that she would not adequately represent the people she had met. She says, "Then various opportunities for becoming involved in social justice issues started to come my way."

Teresa joined an organization at her school called Seeking Education Equity and Diversity. As a student, she did not have money to give to causes she believed in, but she could volunteer her time for coordinating activities and speaking at events.

When Teresa looks at her own life, she feels that the teachings of the Catholic Church back up her passion for serving others and creating a more just world. "We're called to make a difference. We're called to make a change."

Teresa continued her involvement with ARK throughout her high school years. While in college, she protested against weapons makers and the School of the Americas. Participation was a way for Teresa to serve others and educate people about social justice issues.

"Jesus reached out to people who were outcasts and weren't part of society, and he challenges each of us to do the same," Teresa says. She names Salvadoran Archbishop Oscar Arnulfo Romero and Mother Teresa as examples of people who dedicated themselves to service.

Although Teresa's Catholic faith challenges her to dedicate her life to service, it also provides comfort in certain situations, as when she was saying goodbye to her ARK friends in Palestine. "When I had to leave, I realized this might be the last time I would see these people, maybe for the rest of my life. It was important for me to have my faith there to back me up and support me. I realized that through God we will always be connected."

Teresa constantly returns to the example of Jesus. "I think it's amazing that the basis of Catholicism is a person who went around and tried to make change. It's an amazing opportunity to have Jesus as the guide in leading my life. He was absolutely amazing; he was revolutionary in his thoughts, his ideas, and the way he lived," she says.

When Teresa looks at her own life, she feels that the teachings of the Catholic Church back up her passion for serving others and creating a more just world. "We're called to make a difference," Teresa says. "We're called to make a change."

Teresa Capecchi looks to the Beatitudes (see Matthew 5:3–11) for direction and inspiration. "The Sermon on the Mount is one of my favorite Scripture passages because it's full of guidelines on how to lead our lives."

tim roemer

When Tim Roemer was a boy, his great aunt, who was a nun, encouraged him to be a priest. "When that failed, she said that being in public service was the next best thing because I could affect so many people's lives in a positive way. I could extend or improve government services by speaking out for the poor and by practicing the Golden Rule."

Tim Roemer, President, Center for National Policy, and Former Congressman

Public service is the road Tim chose. Many of the decisions he has made in his political career, as well as in other aspects of his life, are rooted in the Catholic faith.

Faith influenced many of the family's activities. "I practiced the social teachings of the Church while I was growing up," he says. "My parents would take us from church to a march with César Chávez, who was trying to draw attention to the plight of migrant workers."

"Those opportunities showed me that Catholicism was not simply about reading a particular verse [in the Scriptures] and memorizing it. Nor was it just about attending Mass on Sunday. It was also about trying to find ways to implement the instructions we read and heard. I treasure those teachings and the fact that [Catholicism] is an action-oriented faith and not just a reflection-oriented one," Tim says.

"Catholicism continues to be extremely important to me in my efforts as a public servant," Tim says. He believes strongly in promoting policies that encourage life. He is in the minority in his political party as a pro-life Democrat, a position he chooses partly because of his faith. "Just as the Democratic Party has been a party dedicated to trying to reduce the number of homeless people, the number of hungry people, the number of people dying of AIDS, I believe the Democratic Party could be instrumental in trying to reduce the number of abortions in the United States. I've tried to articulate both pro-life positions and policies that encourage choosing life."

> "I treasure those teachings and the fact that [Catholicism] is an action-oriented faith and not just a reflection-oriented one."

One area in which Tim worked while in Congress was improving education. He says education is the first step toward succeeding in life. "Too many children in the United States do not have equal opportunities in education or career options later on in their lives."

When Tim has to make decisions that are difficult and unpopular, his faith encourages him. "There have been times when I've cast a vote on a particular issue or given a talk on a particular subject for a crowd and faced opposition. During those times, I've relied on my faith and my confidence in my faith."

"Catholicism continues to be extremely important to me in my efforts as a public servant."

Sometimes the example of other Catholics helps Tim face difficult decisions. "I am always looking for people to teach me how to show leadership, compassion, and courage with other people," Tim says. He acknowledges that the Church has made mistakes, but he knows it has also provided him with positive role models.

Tim attended the University of Notre Dame. He refers to former president Fr. Theodore Hesburgh as "someone who has made significant contributions to higher education, civil rights, and religion. He spoke out on civil rights issues as a Catholic priest in the sixties and seventies, when it wasn't popular. I greatly respected that," Tim says. "Pope John Paul II was a world leader who helped bring down communism and encouraged a new government in Poland. Mother Teresa almost single-handedly helped tens of thousands, or maybe hundreds of thousands, of poor people in India. It's hard sometimes in today's modern world to think one person can make a difference, but there are people in the Catholic Church who have made a difference in the way they have lived their lives."

Tim tries to make a difference in his family life as well as in the public arena. "First and most important, I try to live out my faith by being involved in my own family and by being a good father and a good husband," he says. He and his wife have four children. They strive to teach their children that each one has an obligation to extend help to those who are poor, hungry, and homeless.

He remembers when the family was getting ready to to go on a walk for the homeless. When his thirteen-year-old son said he would like to donate forty dollars, Tim and his wife tried to dissuade him from offering so much. "He looked at us very sincerely and genuinely and said, 'You both teach us this is the most important thing we can do — to help others in need. Why shouldn't I give this much?' It was a pretty convincing argument for a thirteen-year-old."

Tim says, "My faith has taught me that there's not just one way of expressing faith."

Tim says, "My faith has taught me that there's not just one way of expressing faith." He believes Catholicism is no better, for example, than Islam or Judaism. The holy books of these religions teach many of the same lessons about how to treat people. "The consistencies are more important to me than the differences."

"I choose to practice the Catholic faith because the lessons of Jesus and the Bible, the teachings of Saint Augustine and Thomas Aquinas, the social teachings of the encyclicals all emphasize the call to help the 'least among us.' My mom and dad always told us, you can go to church on Sundays but if you don't practice the teachings and live out your faith on Mondays through Saturdays, then you're not adequately acting on your faith," Tim says. "We're put on God's earth for a specific set of days or years or decades. We should try to leave the world a better place and try to influence others' lives. This seems to me to be a pretty important goal."

claire mugavin

Claire Mugavin is an explorer. Although she was raised Catholic and has always considered herself Catholic, she recognizes that she can still learn a lot about the faith. "I find a great richness in my faith. I find that it motivates and informs my life and gives me a belief system and a place of community."

Claire Mugavin, Program Coordinator, Georgetown University

Although Claire feels confident in her beliefs, she has learned that there are more parts of the Catholic faith to explore. She felt lucky to begin her career by working at Xavier University in Cincinnati (where she also attended school) because she knew a lot of young Catholics there who were also practicing and discovering their faith.

She often went to Mass with her friends. "That sense of community is really sacred because with my generation, people are moving and changing. There's so much transition that community is really important."

Claire encountered community in a different way when she spent a semester in Nicaragua. She did service work and studied economics, Spanish, and liberation theology. In Nicaragua Claire observed Christian base communities, which are groups of people that formed in the 1980s during the civil war. The groups gathered to read the Gospels together and discuss how the teachings of Jesus applied to their lives in their country.

"It was amazing to see these men and women, who were poor by economic standards but rich in faith, closeness to God, and understanding of the Scriptures," Claire says. "They used their faith to change their government and their country from within the Church and to empower themselves. I think this is the basic teaching of the Gospels. The Scriptures can help us understand our current reality and see how we can make the world better."

> "That sense of community is really sacred because with my generation, people are moving and changing. There's so much transition that community is really important."

After that semester, Claire took a class on Catholic social teachings. She learned that "the Church supports things that I feel strongly about, things such as the preferential option for the poor, human dignity, and the care of creation."

She has discovered in the lives of the saints that they, like other humans, had temptations and doubts. "The truth is that the saints lived full lives, and in that fullness they found God and grew closer to God and were able to bring good into the world," she says.

> "I'm inspired when I realize that we can bring about peace and justice in this world and that my faith can be a tool for that endeavor."

Claire learned about her namesake, Saint Clare, on a pilgrimage to Assisi and Rome. Claire felt called to understand "how being named Claire connected me to this woman, Saint Clare, who was one of the first women to write and to form her own order for nuns."

Claire lives out her faith daily through her job and through prayer. "I don't think of prayer necessarily as sitting at home, being quiet, and rehearsing in my mind something that has been taught to me. I see my life and the way I live it as a prayer. If I smile at a person who maybe no one has smiled at during the day—that's a prayer. If I purchase things that are made in a dignified way that respects human dignity—that's a prayer."

As she grows in faith, Claire is also building a greater understanding of the sacraments, especially the Eucharist. She likes being a Eucharistic minister. "I recognize that the Body of Christ is in the bread I'm giving to others, but I also see the Body of Christ as being within each person."

There are things that happen in the Church that Claire does not like. "When I first got back from Nicaragua, I was dismayed by the wealth and power the Catholic Church has attained. I would go to Mass and see the golden chalices and stained-glass windows. I realized how much money had gone into the church building, and I thought about how that money could be better spent for the poor. That really frustrated me. However, I sought out and found places that were speaking to the call to serve the poor," she says. "I tried to have a sense of understanding and a sense of listening to the different experiences of people within the faith. The word *catholic* means 'universal,' so there's a place for all of us."

Claire definitely feels that she has found a niche when she works on social justice issues. "I'm inspired when I realize that we can bring about peace and justice in this world and that my faith can be a tool for that endeavor," she says.

Claire Mugavin read Thomas Merton's *The Seven Storey Mountain* (Harcourt Brace, 1948) and Dorothy Day's *The Long Loneliness* (Harper and Row, 1952). These authors inspire her because they had questions and struggles just as she does.

8

catholicism is my heritage

"It's in every breath I inhale. It's deep inside of me. It's in my bones." The sentiments are similar for the many people who were baptized as infants and raised in Catholic families and communities. They cannot imagine life without their religion. It is ingrained in family and community celebrations; it is something they cannot separate from who they are.

bill gullickson

Bill Gullickson grew up in a Catholic world. "I saw my grandma live the Catholic faith for years and years and years," he says. His whole family history has been associated with the Church. He feels it is a special heritage that has been passed on to him, a heritage he has drawn upon often.

Bill Gullickson,
Retired Major League Baseball Player

Some of his childhood memories are wrapped up in sacraments and feast days. First Communions and Confirmations were a big deal in his family, as was Easter. He was an altar server at early-morning Mass as a child. "I used to love to get up and walk to church to serve at the 6:30 a.m. Mass," he says. With few people in the church so early, it was a special time.

After living in Chicago and Minnesota, Bill and his family moved to Tennessee. He was surprised to discover that not everyone was Catholic in his new town. But he learned that God was the common denominator among all religions, and he was content with his Church. "I've always found peace with it," he says.

Bill pitched his first major league baseball game when he was twenty years old. He spent much of his career with the Montreal Expos and was elected to the Canadian Baseball Hall of Fame. He retired after playing for seventeen years. "I had children at home, and I wanted to come home and raise my kids," Bill says. "I played with too many guys who [stayed in professional baseball] until they were older. They had a lot of money and a lot of fame, but their kids were [grown] and gone."

When Bill was forty-six, he experienced a health crisis. He had to draw on his life-long faith to get through it. After an operation, Bill developed a pulmonary embolism and then a bleeding ulcer the size of a golf ball. He went into emergency surgery so doctors could remove his stomach. He died twice on the operating table.

> "I used to love to get up and walk to church to serve at the 6:30 a.m. Mass. With few people in the church so early, it was a special time."

"I had an out-of-body experience: I was above the table looking down, but I didn't see any light," Bill says. "It was like I was a fly on the wall. I looked around and I saw everything that was going on in the whole hospital. Then I looked out into the waiting room and there were all my kids and my wife, all my brothers and sisters and my mom and dad."

> "Right there something came over me and I thought, 'I've got no control over this. I'm going to trust in God, who will watch over me.'"

Bill made it through the operation. He was on life support for six days.

"When I woke up in the hospital, the doctor came in and told me what had happened. Right there something came over me and I thought, 'I've got no control over this. I'm going to trust in God, who will watch over me.' I don't know how anyone who doesn't have faith can go through something like that."

"I had nowhere else to turn. My stomach was cut wide open. I had staples everywhere and tubes down my throat, and my hands were tied to the bed. I was looking around, thinking: 'There's no other show in town. It's just me and God'."

Bill believes it is when people are at the lowest point that God often does something to get their attention. "I look back on that time and realize that God brought me to a certain point, where it was just me and God," Bill says.

Though he now gets his nourishment through a feeding tube, Bill says life is great. "I'm more aware of people in my life. I believe that things don't just happen; they happen for a reason. It's a peaceful feeling that I've found," he says.

Part of the contentment comes from sitting quietly, thinking, and reading—things he would not have done in such a leisurely way before, when his life was filled with so much else. He feels less stress in his life now. He does not worry about yesterday or tomorrow but lives in the present. "I enjoy what God has given me." As for his faith, Bill says he is still learning a lot of things about the Catholic religion. He feels as though he is becoming more educated about his faith, and he likes that. He knows his children might test other religions, even though their heritage is Catholic. But that is okay. Bill says, "God will watch out for us."

During his fourteen years in major league baseball, Bill played for the Montreal Expos, Cincinnati Reds, New York Yankees, Houston Astros, and Detroit Tigers. He had a career total of 162 wins and 135 losses. His best win-loss percentage was in 1991, when he won twenty games and lost nine for the Detroit Tigers.

aggie noonan

In 1785 a group of Catholics from Baltimore set out on a flatboat to find a new home for themselves on the Ohio River. They journeyed to New Hope, Kentucky, where they founded the first Catholic Church west of the Allegheny Mountains. Those people and that journey are part of Aggie Noonan's heritage.

Aggie Noonan,
Nurse and Director of Religious Education

"I feel as though I'm Catholic in my bones. I grew up in a rural area of Nelson County, Kentucky, where everybody was Catholic. I think I stay Catholic because of that and because a lot of my identity is tied up in being Catholic. It's just who I am."

"There is a great pioneering spirit in the Catholics who settled that area, and they have a rich tradition. I think it's tied to the pioneer spirit here in Kentucky."

An important aspect of pioneer life and of Catholicism is community. Aggie has embraced this aspect throughout her life, from the days when she attended Catholic schools, sent her own children to Catholic schools, and worked for the Church as a director of religious education. "I find the sacramental life of the Church to be very, very rich," she says. She describes the sacramental life as "The coming together of people you know and people who care about you and the bringing of your gifts and your brokenness to the table. It requires a certain amount of vulnerability and an acknowledgment that we're not perfect, yet we all have gifts. Being able to come together and celebrate is really important."

Aggie knows that kind of coming together well because she has been a member of the same parish for thirty years. She feels blessed by the people in her faith community who have been with her "through the thick and the thin."

Aggie knows that kind of coming together well because she has been a member of the same parish for thirty years. She feels blessed by the people in her faith community who have been with her "through the thick and the thin."

She also likes the sense that her community has a long and checkered history, because, she says: "That's life. Life is full of mistakes and joys and all sorts of people. I love the sense of universality of Catholicism. I love the fact that you can be really far to the left and really far to the right and still be Catholic. Catholics come in all flavors, so to speak. I think the diversity is good—hard at times, but good."

> "I love the fact that you can be really far to the left and really far to the right and still be Catholic. Catholics come in all flavors, so to speak. I think the diversity is good—hard at times, but good."

Aggie acknowledges that the modern Church has faced a number of difficulties that might push some Catholics to think about leaving the Church. Because of the community she finds in the Church, leaving has never been an option for her.

"It's the sacramental life, the striving to come together as a community, the striving to be more aware of God working in our lives that keep me here."

One way Aggie feels God working in her life is when she feels a call to respond to the needs of others. She has done that in a variety of ways, including working at a Catholic girls' school. She also values the way her faith affirms and celebrates life.

Aggie draws strength from those things as well as from the rituals and liturgies of the Church. She has found her faith to be especially important "in times of extreme tragedy and extreme joy. That's when I most appreciate my Catholic faith."

Aggie's friends sometimes ask her why she continues to be a Catholic when the Church has so many problems. She says: "It's like being on a boat. I stay to bale the water." To her, baling the water as the Church evolves is okay.

"The one thing I've tried to tell my kids and young couples is to try to find a faith community and to bond with it. It doesn't have to be a perfect community. It doesn't have to fulfill all of your needs. In fact, it may be the other way around: It may be that the community really needs you."

adriana trigiani

Adriana is Italian American. Her faith developed as she grew up Catholic in a culture that was intertwined with the Church. Many Italian holidays, and traditions are built around the Church calendar. "We make particular foods on certain holidays and these traditions are woven into the fabric of our family life."

Adriana Trigiani, Bestselling Author

To Adriana Trigiani, faith is a "living, breathing way of life. We live in a dangerous world. Perhaps the world has always been dangerous, but when a person can walk in faith, without fear, that's very freeing."

The Catholic community is the place where Adriana learned to pray. "In times of doubt, I pray. In joyful times, I say a prayer, and when help is needed, I instinctively pray," she says. "Faith is not a concept reserved for special occasions, but rather, a mainstay of everyday life. I pray more since I've become a mother, if only to shout out to God, because I find parenting so humbling and complex."

The spiritual nature of Catholicism is the most compelling aspect for Adriana. "The unseen. The promise of everlasting life. The idea that forgiveness is more important than any particular sin. The concepts of inclusion, redemption, and hope are what keep me Catholic."

Institutions are not always open to change and can get weighed down in rules. They are run by people with imperfections. But beyond that is the soul, which is eternal. "I keep that in mind when I think about religion," she says. "Human beings don't speak for God. We hope that in our prayer life, we are speaking to God. Religiosity can be quite corporate and off-putting; spirituality, however, doesn't have boundaries or judgments, and that's where my heart is."

> The Catholic community is the place where Adriana learned to pray. "In times of doubt, I pray. In joyful times, I say a prayer, and when help is needed, I instinctively pray."

Though people are imperfect, some people make Adriana proud of her Catholic faith. She likes to recall the life of Pope John XXIII. "He came from a poor family near Bergamo, Italy, the area from which my mother's family came. His ideology should be studied because he was about love and was instinctively a uniter, not a divider." Adriana supposes that if he had lived longer (he died in 1963), Pope John XXIII would have pushed for even more sweeping changes in the Church, built a more ecumenical spirit, and led the Church to a more spiritual place.

> "The one thing I learned in Church that has stayed with me is that there is nothing that is unforgivable —nothing— if I am truly penitent."

Adriana wishes more people would incorporate the concept of love and the words of Jesus more deeply into the way they live. She acknowledges that following the ways of Christ, such as not judging people, is difficult. But the reward is invaluable.

"The one thing I learned in Church that has stayed with me is that there is nothing that is unforgivable—nothing—if I am truly penitent. That's a very spiritual concept, one that grows in meaning as I go on in life. Maybe that's why I'm still here."

"I wish we would listen to the words of Jesus and truly make him our homeboy (as the T-shirt says)," says Adriana Trigiani. "So much is said in the name of Jesus and there's so much strife because every religion wants to own Christ and make him an icon for its interpretation of his life. I always remember that because Jesus was Jewish, I am Jewish too, although by way of a long line of Judeo-Christians!"

lynn alcantara

Growing up in the Philippines, Lynn Alcantara did not know any religion but Catholicism. Her grandparents passed the religion on through the family. Lynn and her siblings went to Catholic school. "When we were growing up, we said the rosary every night."

Lynn Alcantara, Social Worker

Lynn now lives in Pennsylvania. Her mother still asks her if she is saying her prayers. She does, although she admits to not saying them as often as she did back home. She misses some of the Catholic traditions that were ingrained in her community.

For example, Lynn grew up saying novenas, which are prayers that last for nine days, and taking part in numerous celebrations at church. Her favorite one takes place during the Advent season, when the community celebrates a nine-day novena. Mass is said each day, and on the ninth day, a midnight Mass is said. "I grew spiritually and saw family and friends during that time," she recalls. "We had our own little community."

> "I grew spiritually and saw family and friends during that time. We had our own little community."

In the United States, Lynn has found a sense of community in her home parish. When people invited her to their non-Catholic churches, she missed the Catholic liturgy, the reading, the homily, the Communion rite, and the blessings.

Working with people who have lost their jobs or homes, or both, and may not have food to feed their families exposes Lynn to many who have far less than she does. "I can do little things and help people a little bit."

One way she helps is by volunteering with the Special Olympics, which holds games for developmentally disabled people. "At first I thought this wouldn't be fun, but after a while I realized that if I do something for an hour and make somebody happy, then it's worth my day."

Her first Special Olympics event was a three-day trip, which included an athletic competition. When one athlete won a gold medal and ran, jumped, and hugged her, she says, "I decided that I'd be here next year."

When Lynn volunteers with the Special Olympians, she receives smiles and thanks for even the smallest things, such as helping an athlete tie his shoes. When she hears participants tell their families about the great trip they had, she is doubly rewarded.

Lynn persists in helping where she can. She also works to strengthen her prayer life and continues to be thankful for all God has given her. She says, "I'm proud to be a Catholic. It's what I know."

For Lynn Alcantara and many other Filipinos, the nine-day Advent novena celebrated in the Philippines is a special Catholic tradition. The Mass begins at dawn each day. Participants demonstrate devotion to the faith and growing anticipation for the coming birth of Jesus. As with other novenas, people believe God will grant special favors to those who celebrate the nine Masses.

liam lawton

Liam Lawton says that in his home country of Ireland, "The omnipresence of God is in all things, much as it is in the North American Indian culture."

Liam Lawton,
Priest and International Recording Artist

That **ever-present** awareness makes Catholicism a natural way of life in Ireland. When Saint Patrick took Christianity to Ireland, it was one of the few instances where a country went through a religious transition without bloodshed. "The transition from one religion to the other was quite easy because Christianity absorbed many of the traditions that already existed, such as respect and awe for natural surroundings," Liam says.

This culture influenced Liam. While he was growing up, his family said prayers together in the morning and at mealtimes and blessed themselves with holy water as they went out the door. Sometimes his mother would shake holy water in the direction her family was traveling.

> "I treasure the sense of community around these gatherings; around these rituals; around funerals, worship services, weddings, and other such gatherings."

"I treasure first and foremost the rituals. I treasure the sense of community around these gatherings; around these rituals; around funerals, worship services, weddings, and other such gatherings. I treasure the language."

When Liam began composing sacred music, he wrote in Gaelic, the ancient language of Ireland. "The language itself, the Gaelic language, was imbued with spirituality," he says.

Liam began writing songs when he was in his teens. He won a number of prestigious song-writing contests and attracted the attention of major recording labels. He gave up a music career to become a priest.

After his ordination, he did pastoral work and taught and directed choirs as he slowly reached again into the world of music. He now devotes himself full-time to music. "I try to honor the gift that has been given to me. I see that as my ministry at the moment," he says.

"There's not a day when I don't thank God. Life could have been very different."

Liam directs music in a cathedral, leads workshops, writes songs, and performs. "I would be the last to believe in myself. It's only because of the belief of others in me. I think people call the gift out of us," he says. "Sometimes we're blind to the gift ourselves, and maybe that's a good thing. If we're too arrogant about it, that becomes a block or barrier."

Like his faith, Liam's music is rooted in his heritage. He draws inspiration from ancient Celtic spirituality. Like any artist, he sometimes worries that the well will run dry. "There's not a day when I don't thank God. Life could have been very different," he says. "I suppose I depend very much on God now. I never know where a piece of music is going to come from, so I pray for inspiration, and it seems to come. I suppose everyone at some time in their lives realizes that."

Besides giving him a rich musical legacy from which to draw, the traditions of the Church in Ireland provide Liam with ways to practice his faith daily. During the twelfth through fourteenth centuries, Celtic life flourished in Ireland. At that time, there were three important aspects of monastic life: prayer, work, and hospitality to strangers.

"I try and reach out to people in whatever way I can. Hospitality is very important," Liam says. The tradition of hospitality grew from the belief that "Christ was the unseen guest who could call at any time in the guise of a stranger."

Although history and tradition are important to Liam, he recognizes that his country and the Church are changing. He calls himself a pacifist and believes that "in the world today, Christianity and the Catholic Tradition have a huge amount to say."

One example of the message is the encyclical on love by Pope Benedict XVI. "We need to examine what it is saying in relation to communities and those who live around us. I think that's the challenge of the Gospel today, to put the message into practice."

"We cannot live in the past."

"We cannot live in the past," Liam says. He likes the analogy of a three-legged stool, with one leg in the past, one in the present, and one in the future to provide balance. He believes that the Church can take elements of what has worked in the past and develop them and examine what has not worked.

"There's such a richness of traditions, smells and bells, sacraments, symbols, rituals. If we can use these vehicles to touch people today, we can become a powerful force for good in the world."

After the 9-11 tragedy, Liam Lawton's recording label received calls from organizations that were gathering music to comfort people. Liam's contribution was "The Cloud's Veil," which includes the following lyrics:

> Even though the rain hides the stars,
> Even though the mist swirls the hills,
> Even when the dark clouds veil the sky,
> God is by my side.

(GIA Publications, *Gather Comprehensive,* no. 619)

saints
encourage us

Throughout its history, the Church has recognized the contributions and miracles of a variety
of outstanding people and has made them saints.
These once ordinary people faced many of the
same struggles we face today. As Catholics look to
the saints, they see models of encouragement and
inner strength.

tara lipinski

When Tara Lipinski attended Saint Thérèse's School as a child, she had no idea how significant the saint would become for her. As a teenager pursuing her dream of Olympic gold in figure skating, Tara discovered that she and Saint Thérèse of Lisieux were alike in many ways.

Tara Lipinski, Olympic Gold Medalist in Figure Skating and Television Actress

"I read about Saint Thérèse and realized I had a lot in common with her. I felt as though I could connect with her. She was fifteen and couldn't make it into the convent when she was fourteen. I couldn't make it anywhere [in the skating world] because everyone thought I was too young," Tara recalls.

Tara's interest in the saint began when a relative gave her a Saint Thérèse prayer card. Although she had grown up Catholic, Tara did not know about novenas, a series of prayers that are usually said over nine days. She learned about one attributed to Saint Thérèse. She began to pray the novena, often receiving signs that her prayers were being heard. For example, she once received roses in the mail on the day the novena promised that something special would happen.

At times Tara would take out a statue of Saint Thérèse to help calm her nerves. She often prayed through Saint Thérèse, asking for little favors. "I believe without a doubt in the power of prayer," she says. "I believe in spirituality. I believe in faith. I believe that faith overcomes so much."

> "I believe without a doubt in the power of prayer. I believe in spirituality. I believe in faith. I believe that faith overcomes so much."

One of Tara's decisions was to go ahead and compete nationally and internationally, even though other people thought she was too young. In 1997 she became the youngest person ever to win the United States National Championship and the youngest ever to win the World Championships.

In 1998 at the age of fifteen, Tara went to the Olympic Games. She wanted to show everyone that she was ready for the competition. She remembers how isolated she felt in the Olympic village and even on the rink, where no one was allowed near her except her coach. Even so, one stranger made it through the barriers. "Right before I stepped on the ice to compete, a little old man gave me a charm necklace with a pink rose on it," Tara says. The rose is one of Saint Thérèse's signs.

Tara won gold, becoming the youngest person ever to do so. It was the year of Saint Thérèse's one hundredth anniversary. "I believed that she was watching over me and helping me. There were little signs. Throughout my whole skating career, I had things like that happen to me."

When it comes to her Catholic faith, Tara says: "I feel very genuine in how I deal with it, especially being in the public eye; I feel very comfortable with it. The best thing about it is that I found Saint Thérèse through it."

Young people, Tara says, "have to find their faith individually." For her, it was through Saint Thérèse. For another person, it might be through another aspect of the Catholic faith. "You take it one step at a time, make your own choices, and find out for yourself."

Since beginning her acting career, Tara Lipinski has appeared in a number of television shows, including *Still Standing*, *Seventh Heaven*, *Sabrina the Teenage Witch*, and *Touched by an Angel*.

bob ketelsen

Bob Ketelsen was not fond of the Catholic Church when he was growing up in the 1930s and 1940s. "When it came to the Church, there was no dissent in the home. It was in the blood, so to speak, and we had to obey," Bob remembers. His parents, however, did not attend Mass because his mother thought her clothes were not fine enough to wear to church.

Bob Ketelsen, Retired Travel Agency Owner, Franciscan Associate, and Volunteer on the Navajo Reservation

Bob was nine years old when his father died. The family fell further into poverty after his death. "We could not afford to put money in the Sunday offering," Bob says. That was significant because the parish listed donors every Sunday. "The Ketelsen name was always at the bottom of the second page, alone, with a zero behind it."

The Ketelsen children, however, attended Catholic grade school and went to daily Mass. Even there they experienced consequences of their poverty. None of the boys [in Bob's family] were asked to be servers. "I do remember always wanting to be up there at the altar," Bob says. "After all, the altar boys would kneel facing the altar and the soles of their shoes would show. We always had cardboard in our shoes because of the holes. I wonder if anyone ever knew how much it hurt not to be asked to be an altar boy."

Bob says that the Church was different in those days, especially for curious people like him who wanted answers about the faith. He once questioned a priest about it, and the response was, "How dare you question the authority of the Church."

> "Ultimately, what helped me was forgiving the Church. I had to release bitter memories of my childhood years for starters. Not an easy thing to do."

In the 1960s, Bob left the Church. "I started on a journey," he says. He attended various churches with friends. Then he began to miss the Catholic faith of his growing-up years. "Ultimately, what helped me was forgiving the Church. I had to release bitter memories of my childhood years for starters. Not an easy thing to do."

"Reading helped me the most. The stories about saints always inspired me, always brought me back to the good times I had in Catholic school and the wonderful nuns who taught me," Bob says.

Bob stayed in contact with those teachers, the Sisters of Saint Francis of Clinton, Iowa. He left his hometown at the age of seventeen to join the navy, and he seldom returned. When he did go home, he visited the convent. The sisters, he says, "always made me feel welcome and remembered me and my brothers and sister. During one of these visits, one of the sisters asked me if I'd consider being an associate of theirs. At first, I said no. After a couple of years of her continuing to ask, I became an associate." (Associates of a religious community are laypersons who share the spirituality and mission of the community.)

> "The stories about saints always inspired me, always brought me back to the good times I had in Catholic school."

When Bob decided to return to the Church in the 1980s, "it was time to come back. I learned about my God. My God doesn't know the words 'thou shall not.' Instead, God is loving and forgiving, telling me always to try again. Don't be hard on yourself; just try again."

Another reason Bob returned was that he saw two good examples in Church leaders: Pope John XXIII in the 1960s and, later, Pope John Paul II. To him, they represented change. Both made public apologies for some of the actions of the Church, and both reached out to all religions.

After he retired from his travel agency business in 1997, Bob put everything he owned in a car and drove to the Navajo reservation, which straddles parts of Utah, New Mexico, and Arizona. He volunteers at Saint Mary's Mission Parish. "I became interested in Saint Francis and his work for the poor. I could relate to the poor, and that got the ball rolling."

The first thing a person notices when walking into Saint Mary's Church, Bob says, is that anyone who is not a Native American is a minority. The second thing is the décor. Native American rugs enliven the space. The scent of smoking cedar is usually wafting through the room.

He enjoys hearing traditional hymns in Navajo. "When the congregation is singing 'Amazing Grace,' I feel the presence of God," he says. Then there is the sign of peace. "This takes time here. It's a social thing. It's what I'm sure our leaders meant for it to be. It's about love."

> "I ask God in the morning to help me get through the day, and I thank God at night."

Bob thinks it is important to share what he believes by example. "I don't pray all the time. I'm not holier than thou. I'm just like everyone else. I ask God in the morning to help me get through the day, and I thank God at night," Bob says.

If Bob disagrees with a teaching of the Church, he shares his opinion. He no longer believes that "dropping out" is the best solution; rather, he wants to be a part of the Church to make changes from within it.

Some religious orders of women have associate programs so laypersons can be affiliated with them. Bob Ketelsen says that being an Associate of the Sisters of Saint Francis of Clinton, Iowa, means, "working with the poor and following the ways of Saint Francis and Saint Clare."

joan rose

Joan Rose grew up with parents who were religious and filled with a strong faith. She remembers praying novenas at church with her mother and watching her mother's lips move as she prayed the rosary.

Joan Rose, Retired Nurse

When young Joan went walking with her father in the Bronx where she grew up, they always made a stop. "We would walk by a church and he would say, 'Let's go on in and say hello to Jesus.' We would stop and pray for a few minutes and then go on our way."

Faith was especially important to the family when Joan's younger sister developed a heart problem. Their mother began to pray through the Blessed Virgin Mary and Saint Jude. "I think he [Saint Jude] was designated by God to be the saint of the impossible," Joan says. "He was someone you could feel very comfortable with." After her sister's problems abated, Joan continued to pray through Saint Jude daily, and she still does.

Today as a retired nurse with children and grandchildren, Joan continues to practice her faith. Although she sometimes has problems with the hierarchy of the Church, she believes in the tenets of the religion and recognizes that those tenets helped form her as a young person and still guide her today.

"I learned all I know from the *Baltimore Catechism*. I learned how to know, love, and serve God. I learned why I'm here: to find out who I am, to find out what my talents are, and to serve others," Joan says.

> "I learned all I know from the *Baltimore Catechism.* I learned how to know, love, and serve God. I learned why I'm here: to find out who I am, to find out what my talents are, and to serve others."

"I truly believe that God knew who I was before I was born, and that I have a purpose here, so each day I do my best to treat people with kindness." If a person lives by the Golden Rule, Joan says, the person cannot go wrong.

The Ten Commandments also provide guidelines for Joan. "Many people believe in the Ten Commandments and they also believe in humanism, but the Church goes beyond that. The two greatest commandments are to love God with your whole heart, mind, and soul and to love your neighbor as yourself. The two greatest commandments are very important."

Joan recognizes that she does not always succeed in living as she wants to, so she asks for help through the Blessed Mother.

> "I believe in this early tenet: 'If you're a Christian, let them see you're a Christian by how you live.'"

Just as Joan's parents drew on their faith to get through the health crisis of their daughter, Joan drew on her faith when her husband faced major health problems. They were living in an RV and moving from place to place, enjoying retirement. While they were in Texas, her husband became ill. Joan thought he was going to die.

She was in a community that was unfamiliar to her. She attended the local church and asked the priest to visit her husband. "The pastor and parishioners helped me as much as they could." Joan needed more than moral support. She lost her credit card and learned she would not receive a replacement card for a month. Two women with whom she had become friends, a hairdresser and a nurse, helped her by cashing her checks. One day when the situation seemed especially frightening, she met her newfound friends in a store parking lot and told them she was not having a good day. The hairdresser said, "We're going to have a prayer circle," Joan remembers. "We held hands in the middle of the parking lot and prayed. I feel that I got a lot of help that day. I believe that if you pray, you will get an answer to your prayer. You may not get the answer you want, but you'll get an answer and you'll get support."

As the health problems continued, Joan and her husband sought refuge at the local chapel dedicated to Saint Jude and prayed through him and the Blessed Mother. Her husband could not sit long enough to attend Mass. "He used to go into the chapel and stand and pray. It gave him a great deal of comfort to go there."

In time, her husband's health improved. Today Joan and her husband live in New York. She takes the Eucharist to a local hospital and leads a Communion service and praying of the rosary at an apartment complex for senior citizens. "I'm meeting sweet little ladies who are probably in their eighties," she says. "Their faith is very, very strong. They have faith in their religion, in themselves, and in others. They are concerned about the world being right. They feel that people of faith need to trust in God and do the very best they can."

"I get up each morning and thank almighty God for giving me my life and for giving me my parents," Joan says. "My faith gives me a sense of purpose in life and helps me to walk on in strength. It helps me to know who I am and where I'm going. It is a guide."

Joan says, "I believe in this early tenet: 'If you're a Christian, let them see you're a Christian by how you live.'"

Saint Jude has had a presence in Joan Rose's life since she was a child. "He was a relative of Jesus and one of the twelve Apostles. He is the patron of desperate situations, because his New Testament letter stresses perseverance in difficult circumstances."

barbara trauth

As a fourteen-year-old, Barbara Trauth did not consider her family to be devoutly Catholic. When her father returned from World War II, the family moved to the suburbs and her father became a successful salesman. "When we moved to the suburbs we were living the American dream. I think both of my parents wanted to leave everything about the war and the Great Depression behind."

Barbara Trauth, Sculptor and Painter

"My parents didn't talk a lot about their faith. There weren't a lot of traditions in the home when I was growing up," she says.

When Barbara was fourteen and the family's seventh child had just been born, her father was diagnosed with multiple sclerosis (MS). The medical community did not know much about this disease at the time. The doctors told her father that he must stay in bed in the hospital. Every night Barbara took care of her siblings while her mother went to the hospital to visit her husband. In time it all became too much for her mother. One evening she had an emotional breakdown.

"That night, my father came home from the hospital. My mom went into the hospital the same evening. I became the chief cook and bottle washer," Barbara says. "I took care of everybody."

A few weeks later, Barbara's mother returned from the hospital. Eventually, her dad went back to work, first using a walker and then a cane. In time, he realized he no longer needed the cane. He went into total remission.

Barbara's faith grew to be a big part of her life. "It's my anchor. I'm probably more spiritual during the difficult times, so sometimes I wonder if God gives me more difficult times so I'll be closer to him."

Twenty years later, when Barbara's father was dying of cancer, he told Barbara more about that awful time. "He was at the point where he was going to lose everything. The bank was going to take our house from us. My mother was hospitalized.

163

They had all these kids. At his lowest point, my father said, 'Jesus, I surrender my life to you if you just let me raise my children.' He was not outwardly a very devout person, but he never had another MS episode. I think that experience is what gave me my initial faith."

Barbara's faith grew to be a big part of her life. "It's my anchor," Barbara says. "I'm probably more spiritual during the difficult times, so sometimes I wonder if God gives me more difficult times so I'll be closer to him."

> One thing that has comforted Barbara during difficult times and brought her answers is praying the rosary. "I've had many true miracles in my life through devotion to Mary. What she does is bring me to her son."

One thing that has comforted Barbara during difficult times and brought her answers is praying the rosary. "I've had many true miracles in my life through devotion to Mary," she says. "What she does is bring me to her son."

One miracle occurred when Barbara and her husband were having problems with their teenage son John, who was hanging out with the wrong crowd. One of his friends died of a drug overdose. John got kicked out of school. He also had drug problems. Barbara thought he needed to re-enter a rehabilitation program, but her husband did not agree.

One evening, Barbara overheard John talking with someone about meeting him at a local store. "I knew John was going to buy drugs from this boy. So I called the street corner drug unit," she says.

At 3:00 a.m., when the deal was supposed to happen, Barbara prayed. "I didn't know what was going to happen. I put my son in Mary's care. I was so terrified."

At 3:05 a.m., the phone rang. It was a police officer, saying that they had arrested the seller. "I wanted my son to be arrested because he needed a reality check." The sergeant did not arrest John, but he did issue a citation for John to appear in court a few weeks later. The judge ordered John to go to a rehabilitation program in Minnesota. He went, but after six weeks, the facility director kicked him out. He was sent to what Barbara calls "a last-ditch place for recalcitrant teens" in Saint Paul.

"It really changed him. It was a conversion experience. There was nothing fancy about it like [the previous places he had gone]. It was down and dirty, in the middle of a ghetto in Saint Paul, Minnesota. Eventually John came home. He went on to complete a double major at Xavier University. He then got a graduate degree in social work, and now he's in law school. He's truly a miracle," Barbara says. "I know that Mary was the one who took care of him."

> "It really changed him. It was a conversion experience. . . . He's truly a miracle. I know that Mary was the one who took care of him."

Today John is devoted to the Eucharist. The Eucharist is also a center point in Barbara's life. She treasures the mystery of Jesus actually being present and "the miracle of the transubstantiation, things that we don't even understand, that Christ is there and that he wanted to be with us, so that's what he left for us, that part of his body, so that we would never be alone."

Another experience that deepened Barbara's faith and encouraged her to get involved in new things was a trip to Medjugorje, in Bosnia-Herzegovina. Since 1981 people have said that the Blessed Virgin Mary has been appearing and giving messages at this place. People who have been there say they have been spiritually strengthened, converted, and healed of physical afflictions. "When I came home, I felt as though I wanted to turn my life upside down," Barbara remembers. "I thought I was faithful before that, but Medjugorje sort of set me on fire. I realized that besides attending Mass and praying the rosary, I wanted to be in a prayer group and I wanted to work in a soup kitchen."

Barbara has now been in a prayer group for sixteen years, and she volunteers in a soup kitchen. She has also been searching for what God is calling her to do as an artist. She pulled together her interest in painting and singing by creating two books based on Handel's "Messiah." That experience so inspired Barbara that she acted on another idea: She contacted the president of Xavier University and shared her idea for a pro-life sculpture. "I wrote him a letter and described the sculpture. He called me and said, 'I want to do this.' It just floored me. I mean, it just bowled me over," Barbara says.

> Barbara still prays the rosary. "I find that the Holy Spirit answers my questions. As I'm saying the rosary, I go to a higher level and I'm guided in what I'm supposed to do with my life."

Barbara created a life-sized, three-figure sculpture. She says it represents "body, mind, and soul, the three areas affected in a woman who has an abortion." The sculpture is now in place on the Xavier campus.

Barbara still prays the rosary. "I find that the Holy Spirit answers my questions. As I'm saying the rosary, I go to a higher level and I'm guided in what I'm supposed to do with my life."

For Barbara Trauth, saying the rosary is like holding Mary's hand.

Barbara Trauth has been especially dedicated to saying the Blue Novena, a fifty-four-day novena attributed to Saint Louis de Montfort. Through a novena, Barbara says, "I have received signal graces." Signal graces are signs sent by God to help people make decisions.

the church is universal

For many people, one of the joys of being Catholic is going anywhere in the world and finding brothers and sisters in the faith. Even if Catholics are praying or singing in a foreign language, the spirit and message of Jesus are there to unite everyone.

tony melendez

For the family of Tony Melendez, the Catholic Church occupied the geo-
graphical as well as the cultural and spiritual center of their lives. "I was
born in Nicaragua, and my parents were always very much churchgoers.
The church was located in the center of the city, and we often gathered
in the plaza."

Tony Melendez, Musician

Even after the family moved to the United States when Tony was a year old, the practices remained at the core of their lives. "My grandfather had a chapel in his house. We would play soccer and the ball would go in there, and he would shoo us out. We always had the influence of having his little chapel nearby."

Tony has come a long way from the kid who ran into the chapel to retrieve the soccer ball. He is now a world-famous musician. His dedication to his faith strengthened after he met Pope John Paul II in 1987 at World Youth Day in Los Angeles.

Tony received a letter inviting him to audition for what he believed would be a two-hundred-person choir that was to sing for the Pope. When he arrived at the audition, he discovered that the event coordinators were looking for a soloist to perform for the Pope. Tony, who was born without arms, played the guitar with his feet.

"I walked away kicking myself," Tony recalls. He had not felt prepared to audition as a soloist. "I thought, 'Dummy, you should have followed up on this letter.' I went home saying, 'Well, they're not going to call me.'"

> "I was twenty-five years old when Pope John Paul II kissed me and told everyone that I was 'hope' and that I needed to 'go out and give hope to others.'"

The organizers had a different opinion; they chose Tony to perform. Recalling the performance that launched him to worldwide fame, Tony says it made him feel more of a responsibility to live his faith. "I was twenty-five years old when Pope John Paul II kissed me and told everyone that I was 'hope' and that I needed to 'go out and give hope to others.' Not just hope, but the message of Jesus in my musical presentations.

I enjoy talking about how much I love [Jesus]. I hope and pray that people feel the realness; it's not something fake or something rehearsed."

> "I feel as though I received a responsibility to say it's okay to be Catholic and to be proud of it."

Tony says he has always been comfortable in the Church and loves the traditions. It was a youth retreat he attended as a teenager, however, that drew him even closer to his faith.

"We were all in a big circle, with a candle in the middle of the room. The priest picked it up and said: 'Each one of you is going to hold this candle, and I would like you to say a prayer. It could be anything.' The Holy Spirit was definitely touching me, especially in hearing the other kids share pains that were very similar to ones I had."

"[The retreat] opened my whole heart up to wanting to be at Mass and to receiving Communion and praying. I wanted to be part of it all," Tony says. That feeling intensified after his performance at World Youth Day. "Since then, it seems that people have asked more of me. I feel as though I received a responsibility to say it's okay to be Catholic and to be proud of it." This responsibility is especially key now that the Melendez family lives in Branson, Missouri, where Catholics make up only six percent of the population.

When there are so few Catholics, Tony explains, people who are not Catholic may have misconceptions about the faith, such as thinking that Catholics worship idols. "It's important that they see me and how much I love my Lord and my Tradition and that I'm not embarrassed to say I'm Catholic."

Now that Tony has attended seven World Youth Days, he has experienced the global community of the Church. "It's amazing to go to different parts of the world and hang out with different Catholics. Praying with them in fields of dirt and receiving Holy Communion. I think that's powerful."

Tony enjoys the Catholic traditions he sees repeated in different ways throughout the world, for example, the various representations of the Virgin Mary. North America has Our Lady of Guadalupe; Poland has the Black Madonna; Portugal has Fátima. The different names commemorate places where Mary is said to have appeared.

"At first you get confused and think, 'Are they talking about someone else?' There are so many different names for Mary. It just goes to show you how people in each area of the world adapt Mary to their culture and how much they love her," Tony says.

He holds dear the richness of the Church's spiritual resources. "We could spend hours and hours studying the writings that are available to us—documents, books, and encyclicals the popes have written. There's so much. Too often we don't take the time to study them and learn from them."

At his concerts, Tony addresses parents, especially fathers, about their role in encouraging faith development. He believes that just as parents earn money and buy food to physically sustain their families, they should also feed them spiritually.

Tony and his wife try to do that with their own two children. Although their children are not growing up with a Catholic church in the town square, they are growing up with parents who hold the faith at the center of their hearts.

Pope John Paul II began World Youth Day in 1984. The event brings together millions of youth and young adults for a pilgrimage experience. Tony Melendez points out, "The biggest youth gatherings I have ever seen are of Catholics."

mary mcnamara

Mary McNamara was aware to some degree at an early age that the Catholic faith is universal. When she sang the song "Faith of Our Fathers," she knew that Catholicism literally was the faith that had sustained generations of her family through tragedies in Ireland. She would never describe her family in Ohio as simply Irish or Catholic; they are Irish Catholic.

Mary McNamara, Social Services Director

At the age of sixteen, Mary had the opportunity to go to Ireland to spend time with various members of her extended family. She learned to pray in Gaelic with her grandparents. She sat with her Aunt Alice by the fire. Suddenly her aunt bowed her head and began to pray. "It was as if she had a rhythm to her day that said it was time for prayer. I was intrigued by that, and I saw how sustaining it was for her. I wanted something like that."

In spite of that desire, Mary thought she had lost her faith as a freshman at Ohio State University. "I started to wonder if I had been spoon-fed all of it. I asked myself whether I believed it." When a friend asked her about her views on abortion, Mary was forced to dig beyond what she had been taught to what she thought about it herself.

As a college student, Mary chose to pursue her Catholic faith. "I wavered for a few weeks, but then I grabbed on and claimed it as mine, not just my family's. I found the Newman Center, and I started teaching Sunday school. I wanted a community, and I found it there."

> As a college student, Mary chose to pursue her Catholic faith. "I wavered for a few weeks, but then I grabbed on and claimed it as mine, not just my family's."

Community has continued to be an important part of Mary's faith journey. Her parish in Cleveland welcomes the homeless, the mentally ill, and others who are often not welcomed elsewhere. Mary helps with the meal the parish serves every Monday.

Mary believes it is important to spend time with people who will listen to her questions and maybe provide answers. "I still go out with two nuns from my high school to a steakhouse every month. I treasure that. I think that is one of my best assets, to have people to walk with me."

Mary encountered some hard questions when she took a trip to Kenya with a foundation that focuses on AIDS and orphans. "It was peer-to-peer learning," Mary says of the trip. It included sixteen professionals. "We went and held babies. The purpose was to be less insulated from AIDS. The trip sure did that."

> She began to think more about what Jesus really meant when he said, "To those whom much has been given, much will be required" (Luke 12:48).

Many questions followed Mary home as she tried to sort through the experience and what it meant to her life in the United States. She began to think more about what Jesus really meant when he said, "To those whom much has been given, much will be required" (Luke 12:48).

During her stay in Nakuru, Mary wanted to attend Mass on Sunday, so she went to the lobby of the hotel to ask about the nearest church. The security guard, Nicholas, walked to the church to find out the Mass times for her. Then he went with her at 6:45 on Sunday morning. While they were walking and talking, Mary discovered that Nicholas was Catholic and had wanted to be a priest. Because he was the only male in his family and only men can inherit property in Kenya, he was not able to pursue that path. But he still valued his faith and was thankful for a spiritual book that Mary passed on to him.

In church, Mary listened to the Mass in Swahili. "I didn't understand the words, but I knew I was part of something bigger. I treasure the global faith of the Church," she said. "I realize I'm so connected."

Part of that connection comes through the common liturgy and traditions of the Church. "I love to sing at Mass and see a ten-year-old singing on one side of me and a seventy-year-old singing on the other side of me. We might be there for different reasons, but the Church makes a place for all of us."

Annual Church seasons such as Lent also connect Catholics. "I treasure the Lenten season, even though I don't do so well at giving up soft drinks or chocolate," Mary says. Mary has found that her faith gives structure to her daily life and guides her too.

"It's hard to hear the voice of God in the world amid all the materialism, but I strive to hear it," she says. "I live out my faith by being joyful, loving [others], and working toward justice in the world. My faith has given me a moral compass that has guided me through my secular work, my political activity, my family."

> "I love the Church for its dedication to social justice and the preferential option for the poor."

A few years ago, Mary's godchild asked her why she was Catholic. She explained: "It's kind of like my car. When I'm on the road driving, we're all going in the right direction and we're all in cars that look different. But my vehicle is the one that's driving me toward God."

Mary says: "The Catholic Church has been delivering Jesus's message for centuries, so I'm willing to stay with it through the challenges. I love the Church for its dedication to social justice and the preferential option for the poor. I like that it's okay to ask questions of the Church. If I leave, that's no good, because I don't have a voice. If I stay, I have credibility because I've been Catholic for thirty-four years." When people ask questions, Mary believes, God gives them grace.

Mary appreciates how Catholicism is so ingrained in her family. "I like that it's so tied to my family history. We're Irish Catholic. I can tie it back forever."

Mary McNamara is part of a small faith group. She and a handful of other people gather for prayer, fellowship, and service. "We have conversations over dinner that are about bigger topics than the weather. We're trying to ask the hard questions and explore them."

mike penich

Mike Penich grew up with an Italian mother and a Croatian father, so it is no surprise that as an adult, one of the things he treasures about the Catholic church is its universality. He attended a Croatian Catholic Church while growing up, and later, a Hispanic church. Today he is the deacon in a parish that serves Asians, Latinos, Americans, and many people who have left their communities to join the Catholic Church.

Mike Penich, Deacon and Retired Principal

"I teach RCIA [Rite of Christian Initiation of Adults]. The Episcopals and Evangelicals bring their heritage to the faith, and I think that enhances it for all of us," Mike says.

Participating in a variety of ethnic customs has also enriched Mike's spiritual life. The Filipinos in the parish celebrate the coming of Christ through Masses during the nine days before Christmas. Mike challenged himself to learn some Tagalog (the native language of the Philippines) so he could speak a few sentences of it at Mass. "When you show respect for other people's cultures, they appreciate it so much," he said.

A custom that deeply touches Mike is a Latino celebration of Good Friday. On this day, Latinos pray a living way of the cross, in which people take on the roles of Jesus, Mary, and others who participated in the Passion. They walk through the street commemorating the events of that day. "It's not like a play. There's a reality to it," Mikes explains. Jesus really carries a cross. He is whipped. He falls. "There are thousands watching in the streets," Mike says. It touches him that the event draws such a crowd.

> A strong force in Mike's everyday life is the love God has for him. "Daily I'm reminding myself that Jesus died for me and he loves me."

Another celebration with a big following is the feast of Our Lady of Guadalupe. "Throngs of people come to the church," he says.

A strong force in Mike's everyday life is the love God has for him. "Daily I'm reminding myself that Jesus died for me and he loves me," he says. When Mike is tired and the phone rings with a call from someone who needs help and what he really wants to do is stay home, Mike says: "I force myself to remember [Jesus's] love for me. We are his hands and feet on earth." Mike offers counsel, drives someone where he or she needs to go, fulfills whatever duty is before him.

Sometimes his ministry affects other parts of Mike's everyday routine. "I go to the gym and ride the life cycle beside the guy who is going through a divorce. I sit in the sauna and talk with someone about how to get an annulment. The Lord gives us so many opportunities every day. When we wake up in the morning, we don't have a clue," he says. God is even in the ironing Mike does for his wife. "I have the time to do this. I'm doing it for her because this is how God wants us to treat one another."

Mike has felt that sort of love coming to him from other people. His mother is elderly and losing her memory. Because Sunday is Mike's busiest day with his responsibilities at Church, parishioners help with his mother on that day.

> "The Lord gives us so many opportunities every day. When we wake up in the morning, we don't have a clue."

"The ladies from the Church take her food and visit with her. It makes it easier for me. It also puts her in good spirits," he says. "It means a lot to know that I'm not in this alone. God's hand is in all of this."

Mike emphasizes that he is not perfect. He fails. He loses patience. But he also knows that "the Church gives us so many opportunities to show our love for God and to receive forgiveness."

In the sacrament of Penance and Reconciliation, Mike finds a great gift for Catholics. "The first thing I do when I'm at Mass is admit to my failures. The door is never shut to us. We always know God loves and forgives us."

When Mike is teaching RCIA, he finds that confession often raises the most skepticism among people who have been in other religions. Mike has seen the skepticism dissolve. "After candidates experience [the sacrament], they talk about the beauty of it," he says.

The beauty, the love, the heritage, and the universality of the Catholic Church are all reasons Mike has remained Catholic all these years. "I believe there is no perfect place on earth, and I find the Catholic Church to be comfortable for me."

While he is celebrating feast days in Wisconsin, Mike is comforted to know that Africans and Asians are celebrating those same feast days in their parishes.

Mike Penich remembers a Marian celebration from his childhood, where parishioners would take the statue of Our Lady of Mount Carmel from the church for a procession in honor of Our Lady on her feast day, July 16. This Italian custom, like others he has learned, illustrates for him the devotion of the people who participate.

Epilogue

I was talking with a major league baseball player the other day who told me, "I always have time for my faith."

It is easy for school, work, family, and friends to become the priorities in our lives. The people I have met through this book have reminded me that when our faith is integrated into our lives, it becomes a part of all the other things, whether we are eating breakfast with family or friends, completing a homework assignment, or attending a sporting event—whatever we are doing.

I often need to remind myself of the many different ways God is continually present in my life. This book presents some of the best reminders I have found.

> "The people in this book have taught me lessons and given me wisdom."

Bishop Houck pointed out that regardless of the messages society gives us, Jesus did not call us to be rugged individualists but rather to be a community.

Bob Lefnesky and Susan Sucher talked about John, chapter 6, so lovingly that I had to read it again. When my Protestant friends express uncertainty about the Catholic interpretation of the Eucharist, I can refer them to this Scripture reading.

Kristen Day reminded me that faith is a commitment, not just something to take for granted.

The people in this book have taught me lessons and given me wisdom. They have piqued my curiosity about my spirituality, Catholicism, and my relationship with God. I hope they have done the same for you.

Acknowledgments

The scriptural quotations contained herein are from the New Revised Standard Version of the Bible, Catholic Edition. Copyright © 1993 and 1989 by the Division of Christian Education of the National Council of the Churches of Christ in the United States of America. All rights reserved.

The quotation on page 75 is from the *Sacramentary*, English translation prepared by the International Commission on English in the Liturgy (New York: Catholic Book Publishing Company, 1985), page 564. Illustrations and arrangement copyright © 1985–1974 by Catholic Book Publishing Company, New York. All rights reserved. Used with permission.

The song lyrics on page 147 are from the refrain of "The Cloud's Veil,"by Liam Lawton, copyright © 1997 by GIA Publications, in *Gather Comprehensive*, second edition, by GIA Publications (Chicago: GIA Publications, 1994, 2004), number 619. Copyright © 2004 by GIA Publications, 7404 S. Mason Ave., Chicago, IL 60638, *www.giamusic.com*, 800-442-1358. All rights reserved. Used with permission.

During this book's preparation, all citations, facts, figures, names, addresses, telephone numbers, Internet URLs, and other pieces of information cited within were verified for accuracy. The author and Saint Mary's Press staff have made every attempt to reference current and valid sources, but we cannot guarantee the content of any source, and we are not responsible for any changes that may have occurred since our verification. If you find an error in, or have a question or concern about, any of the information or sources listed within, please contact Saint Mary's Press.

Photo Credits

Anne Rice picture by Sue Tebbe.
Representative Wayne picture by Bud Kraft.

Place Your Photo Here

Why do you choose to be Catholic?

Place a Friend's Photo Here

Why do you choose to be Catholic?

Yes! We Are Catholic

Place a Friend's Photo Here

Place a Mentor's Photo Here

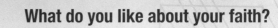

What do you like about your faith?

"Some people say that when you pray, your prayers aren't answered, but I'm a living witness that they are."

—Paula Davis, housekeeper, Xavier University

"I love that [the Church] goes back to the Last Supper. I love that it's a mystical religion, very prayer and meditation oriented."

—Catherine Hicks, actress